The Films of Greta Garbo

The Film:
GRE

of

TA GARBO

by Michael Conway, Dion Mc Gregor, and Mark Ricci
with an introductory essay by Parker Tyler

THE CITADEL PRESS   SECAUCUS, NEW JERSEY

ACKNOWLEDGMENTS

The authors wish to extend their thanks to the following for their generous loan of photographs for this book: Gerald D. McDonald, Paul Nemceck, Carlos Clarens, and the Museum of Modern Art.

Other photographs were supplied by Culver Pictures, Monkmeyer Press Photo Service, and the Memory Shop.

Seventh paperbound printing, 1980

ISBN: 0-8065-0148-0

Contents

The Garbo Image

The Garbo Image

by PARKER TYLER

Garbo. This will not be a drooling piece about her. But just to speak her name, or write it, is to evoke what I would call, after much brooding on the subject, a presence in a Madame Tussaud's of the imagination. The world we live in, where fame is a white heat perpetuated by a labyrinth of mirrors, engenders that sort of imagination in all of us . . . in all of us except, perhaps, Garbo. Greta Garbo would never undergo the hot-wax masking that makes for lifelike accuracy if your image is going into Tussaud's. For all I know, her image is already there, although I don't recall seeing it during my first and only visit to that attraction. Since Tussaud's is the most horrible place in which I've ever seen the human being imitated at full length and in clean three dimensions, I soon fled in disgust. When, on a flight of stairs, I ducked under the rope regulating upgoing and downgoing traffic, a guard standing by was so shocked he tried to restore the proper order of things. But I was adamant. Tussaud's is the world reincarnated as surface truth and nothing but.

This is the scandal of Tussaud's, whether regarding fame or notoriety: its total, alienating worship of *surface* facts. It is a world meticulously purged of all humor. Garbo was a woman who had everything but—yet the "but" does not imply she lacked humor. Surface signs in anyone, even false eyelashes, a beard, the roles assumed by actors, are mere indications of things within; they never represent only flesh, hair, face powder, lipstick, fashion "accessories." However much artifice is present, it is "trued" by the apparent aim. Garbo as an actress was a fabulous chameleon. Notice, in this book, how much a hair-do alone can transform her in person and in mood; also, how

much severity is communicated by her profile in contrast with her fullface. With a younger woman facing her, she automatically assumes an extra, rather masculine, dignity: something removed and enigmatic. This characteristic may be enhanced by the corners of her mouth, which take a deep dip when she assumes a solemn expression. Yet how much girlishness she could call into her face, as so many illustrations here attest! In her last film, *Two-Faced Woman,* she looks at times like a matron who has decided to reduce—and succeeded. Yet even at this last stage of her acting career, she could call forth youth, at will, from face and body.

Moral and emotional aims have their own transitions in individuals. Part of the art of acting is to reflect the difficulty of these changes, which raise important questions in human affairs despite the individual's identity, including his sexual identity. At a crucial moment of Shakespeare's *Hamlet,* its hero makes a complex play on terms of identification when King Claudius calls himself, "thy loving father, Hamlet." Hamlet catches him up: "My mother—father and mother is man and wife, man and wife is one flesh; and so, my mother." Notice the singular verb—the *only* verb in the sentence although the subjects are plural and of different sexes. No bagatelle, that paradox . . . Kenneth Tynan paid it considerable heed when he announced to the reading (and seeing) public that Garbo—Mr. Tynan said it with obvious relish—is "a girl."

Indeed? As if that were all she was, and is, or has grown to be. There are more sexes, and sexual nuances, than can be counted on the fingers of two hands. At first glance, Mr. Tynan could have meant, jokingly, only one thing: a gallant sort of authentication; gallant, but also gratuitous. There has been an immense amount of joking about Garbo's sexual personality since it came to exist for everyone on the screen. The theme of sex (at least in journalism) is inexhaustibly humorous. Some of the jokes are nice (I mean witty). Others are not. Yet sexual jokes are perhaps the finest measure of vulgarity of mind and feeling in the world. We seldom note this truth as such, but think how it pervades our lives and thoughts, how many "incidents" it causes. . . . Man and woman, like father and mother, simply *is.* As usual, we find Hamlet's "aberrations" an index to the continuous stream of human experience.

Garbo? Yes, Garbo is an object of interest which, dressed like a woman, can still create—meek and mild as she is—a public stir. One is prompted to say the stir is her own fault. If she always smiled into news cameras, if she didn't throw up her arm as if warding off a blow, if she didn't feel touchy about her slouchiness, there wouldn't be so much zeal about trapping her image, so much zest in scrutinizing it. Garbo's war with the press, a cold war started in Hollywood soon after she arrived there, has gone on and on, maintained by something so real in her nature that it is like an ancient, if bloodless, feud to the death. Its mode can be, on the other hand, both peaceful and polite on the surface. If a celebrity enters a bookstore, he or she must assume a minimal interest aroused in customer and clerk. I heard of one such incident from a firsthand witness.

Miss Garbo was unmolested. She usually is in this, one of the very top-level bookstores. "Miss Garbo" is approached by clerks as every other customer is. Yet on this particular occasion, the rumor had an electric underground life: her presence was hailed in silence by customers sidling closer, heads popping up over bookstalls, tactful cranings of the neck from behind pillars. It isn't the excitement of such occasions (at least, when no cameras are around) but the *suppression* of excitement that stamps them. Almost any other celebrity, or would-be celebrity, betrays his self-conscious effort to be unself-conscious when in public places. Not so Garbo. She is obviously a trained self-suppresser: a woman who "won't" in multitudinous and indefinable, but ineradicable, ways. Well-preserved (I know, because I casually happened to meet her socially) for someone just under sixty, she has little cause to bemoan the wrinkles and bags, to try desperately to prestidigitate them away through artifice. I should say she takes a normal care for street appearances and all appearances outside her home. She was dressed neatly and plainly when seen, as I mentioned above, in the bookstore; she does not always wear the dark glasses and the wide, floppy hat or broganish low heels. Almost any woman her age wants to shade her eyes from light directly above. Arriving unexpectedly with a party attending a semi-private film screening about three years ago, she wore a dark suit, little or no makeup and an inconspicuous, though eye-shadowing, hat. She struck me as somewhat like a tamed beast, used to tolerating a cage with other beasts, but with an habitual, deathless reflex of caution. In the world, she just won't follow a script, and least of all the social script laid out by surviving professionals, retired or unretired. Maybe you could call her "entrances" things of understatement. But her acting had that, too, if one pauses to think of it. Her body had power and length for a woman's body and these, for reasons of the script, were best if understated. One sees the wisdom. Garbo on the screen was destined to go far beyond techniques both old and new as prescribed for the Fatal Woman, beautiful and drenched in glamor. Look how she puts her fist down on the table in *Anna Christie*—and the brutal decision signified in the same shot by her squared shoulders. Not that, at first anyway, her character-transformations always worked: For Garbo the ridiculous and Garbo the willowy, see different guises of her in *The Torrent*. In substance, she carried on the disqualified Vamp tradition with a subtlety, distinction and horsepower that do stack fantastically, if you stop to tote them up.

I've taken occasion to tote them up, myself, in many impulsive ways. Now I rather think those ways were *too* impulsive. I once referred (a phrase that found its way into print via Cecil Beaton's impetuous pen) to her "monosyllabic pelvis," a description I could justify now, or when I wrote it about 1937, only with the most abstruse reasoning. I was playing a variation on the even-then common theme of Garbo's arrestingly ambivalent sort of sexuality. I realized this well for I also wrote then that she had "the long, poetically prehensile arms of a growing youth." With guile, I did not say whether of boy or girl; nominally, of course, "youth" in the singular implies the male. Like Hamlet, who allowed his Ophelia to go by the board, I felt youth (or age) to mean man *and* woman.

Let there be no mistake. My point has nothing to do—God forbid!—with bisexual or any other kind of sexual practices. Nor did Hamlet's. Many such practices are typically, if unpardonably, associated by the mass public with naughty sex masquerade, especially when not technically for theatrical display. Garbo was, every inch of her, an *actress;* for that reason, she is very much a girl and has grown to be, I imagine, something of a woman, too. I think she was quite a woman in her screen roles, even while I am not the first to have noted that she just naturally appealed to men, women and children alike. A magical exemption hovers about the head of anyone, no matter of which sex, of whom that can truly be said. They can take any form they like, these prodigious and likeable zanies. Zeus did, and most people found him irresistible—never forget that "rape" has a long history as a puritanical synonym for what is sometimes sudden and tardy consent. Of all actresses of whom I have any knowledge in the theatre, she was by far the most mercurial; I mean she just naturally, under certain conditions, transformed herself. She was always "Garbo," to be sure. Yet in certain views—find them and see—she could look like the newest starlet of the present day, like Deborah Kerr, or like the mannish, straight-haired, long-bobbed horsewoman she was in one portrait. In abbreviated sports togs, in *The Single Standard,* she looks neither chic nor impossible. Yet I think a bathing suit was literally the only thing that made Garbo camera-shy.

One of the funny things about the professional stage act by female impersonators (or male impersonators) is the surprisingly instantaneous attraction it has for the sex impersonated and the sex impersonating; as something informal and impromptu—I mean social, not professional—the idea is sometimes snapped up then and there, and the resultant transformation is the more heartwarming, the more absurd and impossible. "Drag acts," I believe, are not confined to the declassé sexes. Garbo "got in drag" whenever she took some heavy glamor part, whenever she melted in or out of a man's arms, whenever she simply let that heavenly-flexed neck—what a magnificent line it makes: like a

goose's rather than a swan's—bear the weight of her thrown-back head. It is a ballerina's art. See it in almost any of her films; I know some version of it must be in all. She took the first chance to show it in *The Story of Gösta Berling* when, as a chaste young wife who has lost her heart to a noble scoundrel, she finds herself offering both hands to Lars Hanson. Usually it is a form of womanly surrender (see *Camille* or *Anna Christie*, *The Kiss* or *The Mysterious Lady*) and if not such surrender as made to a man, then languid surrender to the weight of a mood; maybe even to the weight of her slavery to Hollywood.

Eventually Garbo owned the best-trained deportment of anybody then in Hollywood films, with the rare exceptions of certain male comedians (among them Chaplin). She could not be beat, not even by Marie Dressler, who didn't compete in the same sort of calisthenics. (By the way, calisthenics is a very respectable term, going far beyond skillful falling yet with no relation to *judo*.) One must concede that Garbo could be awkward, largely because nature had ordained she could never be "dainty," as all *sweet* American star actresses had been. Yet no matter how you have to take Garbo, her screen image has the girthiness associated with goddesses. The very width of her hips (note it in a scene from *Susan Lenox*) was a majestic thing. On the other hand she had to be careful of her projecting angles; they were far apart, for female extremities, but with time she learned to manage them all: the shoulders, wide as Aphrodite's; the hands, invariably expressive; the feet, long as those archaic Greek fragments that are mostly pedestal and are cut off at the ankles. It was necessary that they *not* be in the picture when she stood in her stockinged feet to equate her height with a leading man's. Just before the "take," her impersonal query would come: "Are the feet in?"

The day had quite passed, as Garbo entered Hollywood's gates, when a Vampire à la Theda Bara (or even that petite and inimitable siren, Alla Nazimova) could thrust any part of her anatomy, sparse or ample, toward a man without thinking twice, or fling herself about in careless, witchlike dudgeon. The film art was being domesticated (gradually) to sense, if not also to sensibility. Garbo always had too much sheer *class* for that kind of exhibition. She just *did*. You see that even in *The Story of Gösta Berling*, in which she had her first leading role in Sweden, before her Hollywood years. Acting became for her a question of finding a style that would control the far bodily points without destroying their articulacy. Reducing the flesh helped, though the flesh was fair, ripe as a fruit, at first. At least, reducing, italicizing the bones and the lankiness and the shallow bosom, made perfection of carriage absolutely *de rigueur* if she were not to suggest, next to some of her leading men, a camel.

Such is the fearsome inquisition of photography. Actually, in

Garbo, the domesticated import, you began to catch sight of a lily, a spray of passion flowers, a gait startlingly like Tallulah's, a neck somewhere between a swan's and a goose's, a flight in the air as of doves. As simple a thing as hunching her shoulders so as to narrow them was part of an inconspicuous scheme to type herself as frail and womanly. Her body learned an infinite variety when it had really been sent to school, and considering all the handicaps put upon it, its recitation of a role was beautiful. Today, women think they have the fashionable droop of the 'Twenties, and even—now that dress designers have just launched the "Garbo look"—the peculiar chic of the swashbuckling numbers from Garbo's long-lasting, off-screen wardrobe. But these women are deceived by externals. Fashion models could, and did, learn things from the young Garbo and from the young Dietrich, who followed Garbo to Hollywood and also became a star of the first rank. These lessons could not then be found in other women, professional actresses or not.

The fashion world has been using Garbo ever since she slimmed down and brought out her idiomatic style. For years now, rakishness, bold angularity (in visible bone and posture), mock insolence (the kind with a Mona Lisa smile), and the insinuation of an apparently uncontrollable pelvis, have been the fashion model's stock-in-trade. Much more came from Garbo of the 'Twenties and 'Thirties than people, through the annual tides of fashion, have supposed. The negligently slung hip, the air of pseudo-helplessness (assumed to "fetch" a man), the cocked elbow and the space-straddle were all Garbo's. I mean they were hers as "originals," not as copies. In her, they were integral with romance, and had nothing to do with current space-sculpture or the man-trap kind of modern machine-sculpture.

There are no more Garbos; or Dietrichs, for that matter. Elizabeth Taylor is the best that the man-trapping tradition of eroticism can do. There must be a reason for this state of things. There was—and nobody knew it sooner than Garbo, the lovely bait! The fact has been publicized, to satiety and beyond, that she soon tired of the glamor profession and wished to portray a plain woman for a change. There crept into the public consciousness, inevitably, that the most luscious siren of all resented her furbelows, preferring, as sneak shots of her indicated, to go about like a lady golfer after a hard afternoon. The streaming, unkempt, shoulder-length hair went with the flat feet, the stride, the scalped eyelids. The reduction of the eyebrow to a minimum presence and the lifting of lid and eyelash to a maximum presence was first a Garbo trait (see the portraits here). The Joan Crawfords and the rest came afterward. The thoughtless but susceptible public inferred the wrong thing from the dramatic contrast between Garbo's professional image and her private one. Garbo's off-screen presence exposed nothing scandalous, but betrayed, rather, what a fabulous medium of transformation the film, like the stage, is.

Everyone who knows Garbo's career can remember her charming girlishness and a silent laughter that had a radiance. Actually, the studio crimped her hair too much—the long, plastic bob that was so much the fashion—till a few tries at smoothing it down and pinning it behind her ears showed how well she responded to the severe. Adrian, her ingenious costumer, took advantage of the opportunity in *Mata Hari* to give her headgear that were luxurious versions of the skull-cap. In the film *Love* she wore a veil-swathed toque and a white fur hat, based on the shako, as if she had been born in them. No star was ever more obviously dressed-up in the clothes-horse sense, or less obviously so in the social sense. If the metallic pants she wore in *Mata Hari*—fitted, of course, but worn under an open skirt—didn't cramp her style, nothing *ever* could have. Adrian's version of the Juliet cap imposed a remarkable test on this star of stars: she wore it slightly awry and with hair hardly showing. Visualize Norma Shearer like that, as Juliet, and you'll know what I mean.

Garbo's insistence is supposed to have induced her studio to let her play those "plain women," Anna Christie and Ninotchka. At any rate, they were two of her most successful parts and O'Neill's heroine a particular test of the star's glamor. Anna is a drab—a good drab, of course, but the victim of men (or so she thinks) and their declared hater. I saw the film again, not long ago, and renewed my acquaintance with the sensation-producing first entrance, for it was in *Anna Christie* that Garbo first spoke—to be *heard*, I mean, as well as to be *seen*. The dusky voice was like a chord on violin strings and it struck an abysmally pathetic note that was as much Garbo's music as Anna's hard luck. The star triumphed and yet there was a difference in her. Something had been subtly dislocated in the focus of her personality.

It would be unjust to claim that she had never worn simple dresses or behaved like a normal, decent woman—if that is not too stiff a phrase for normal, decent women—but no female star, unless we except Jean Harlow, can have a career by playing fallen women of a cheap kind. The public did not have to be told Garbo really had, beneath Anna's tawdriness, a conspicuous heart of gold, or even that Anna as a character was really Eve behind the "hard luck." The public already believed it of Garbo and every other movie heroine it favored. *Hard luck* is always the criminal where sentiment rules. And sentiment, in the mass public, always rules.

So much for Garbo as a plain woman. Or perhaps one should say: a plain-clothes woman. For there was a moralistic strategy in her stubborn desire to play someone stripped of all frills: the bait was the man-trap and the man-trap's bait was the allure of—frills: the greasepaint, the glitter, all that we call woman's wiles to make herself sexually desirable. "I vant to be alone." This is one of the legendary gags by which Garbo's public abused her sacredness. Yet it might be a line of Anna Christie's. There *are* times when many of us, male or

female, want to be alone . . . and demand it, if compelled to, as a right. But Garbo as the typed heroine never wanted to be alone; she always wanted to be with a man, even if it was more her destiny than a simple desire, and even if it was only to ruin the men and perhaps herself too. If she voluntarily gave up a man, as in *Camille,* or was deprived of him, as in *Mata Hari,* or ultimately committed suicide for having yielded to him, as in *Anna Karenina,* it was all for love; and love without plumage is not wholly understandable to the world at large. A "chick" must have plumage; a chick, to take the metaphor more seriously, seems born to have plumage. Doesn't the male bird woo the female with plumage, among other things? And isn't this entirely within nature's pattern? And so on . . .

Garbo somehow, for whatever obscure reasons, didn't see it that way. It is part of her whimsical story to prefer plumage where nature has, in the most literal sense, really put it; that is, on *birds.* So it seems from a story told by Aldous Huxley to Basil Rathbone and repeated by the latter in his recently published autobiography. Huxley, allegedly, was once summoned personally to Garbo's presence to be informed, says Rathbone, of the nature of a script she wished him to write for her. Her friend Mercedes de Acosta was present, according to Huxley, and after a portentous pause, Garbo declared she wished to act the role of St. Francis of Assisi: the script was to be about this saint distinguished for his love of birds and animals. It would have meant a transformation to challenge all Adrian's powers. One can visualize his variations on the cowl, and the coiffures alone would have led to new triumphs for star and designer. Yet this was not the aspect that immediately struck Huxley, who allegedly burst out with: "What? Replete with beard?" Like most of the stories about Garbo, this one has its crude comedy.

This comedy was part of the persecution Garbo earned because, by the time she had become a great romantic heroine (great enough to make an audience audibly weep), and been a great romantic heroine over and over, the mystery of the Sphinx had evolved from being altogether fascinating to being slightly offensive. As I implied above, Garbo knew all these things before her public did, and even before her studio did. It was as if *the birds* had told her. Through the years, she had chafed at an injustice in her professional destiny: an injustice that was born, probably, in that distant New York summer, during which she had stewed while Mauritz Stiller, who had made her a condition of his contract with M-G-M, tried to persuade that studio that she had a big future. It is very hard to think of Garbo as anything but Garbo: the smooth siren with the high style, the induplicable features and the induplicable gestures. But *everyone* has another self; everyone "is" his own mother and father, as well as vice versa. Something in Garbo wanted to be where sex wasn't. For if there's sex, there's bound to be sex's uniform; if there's a uniform, there's bound to be a costume, and if there's a costume, there is, possibly, masquerade. And if there's masquerade, there's a kind of deception.

No, I won't say Garbo always wanted to be Garbo and had to be always someone else. She was always Garbo. It was simply a question— and what suspense this could create!—of *which Garbo* she would be next. It was like choosing a dress from a wardrobe, a shade of lipstick, a jewel . . . Garbo could have had practically anything she asked from her studio, providing, of course, it was not a role that showed too "different" a Garbo. Then came *Ninotchka.* "Garbo laughs," said the ads, as, before that, the ads had said, "Garbo speaks." Had her adorers really *missed* the belly laugh she finally provided in *Ninotchka?* I found the film very boring and Garbo herself without the sting she used to have. It wasn't that she was really being the "human," "light-hearted," "down-to-earth" woman that was the gimmick of the part. It was that she was ceasing to take her acting seriously. The art of Hollywood as an essentially inferior thing could not have escaped a woman as generally intelligent as Garbo. Her destiny was to contribute an actress-personality to the films. That destiny had become monotonously fulfilled and was dying on its feet, quite unsmiling.

Many a private tear, many a confidential pang and grimace, must have been spent on this fact by Garbo, who was the first to realize it. Her friends must have tried to console her by urging her to go on seeking new roles. In Ninotchka, the Soviet citizen, whose mind has to be taken off Communism in order to make her aware of "love," a new role *had been* found—but Garbo, instead of filling it, seemed to drain it. It had remarkably little juice . . . just *how* little grew clear from its immediate successor, *Two-Faced Woman,* a film so heartlessly barren and false to any real significance that it became the death-knell of the star's career. There was no more Garbo, except for the wolves who feed on celebrities.

Garbo "became" a star who had retired, as it were, under suspicious circumstances. It seemed not to be for love or from disgust with life, for she neither married, disappeared from the world nor committed suicide. Her romances now were, in a rather ominous sense of the word, past. Being a Fatal Woman might have been construed to have reaped its bed of thorns. We have to reckon with the whole meaning of the myth of illicit love when we consider Garbo's case. She was the image of a woman who had lived for love and given everything for it except the blood in the veins of the actual woman, Greta Garbo. And yet no one, I would seriously hazard, ever particularly believed that Garbo led a secret love life: one that was bitter, and passionate, and pathetic, and ironic, and sometimes self-defeating—as it was in her films.

She was successful! She was a *star!* When a Marilyn Monroe

quenches the flame of life, however involuntarily, the event has been prepared for by a whole series of publicized difficulties and near-breakdowns in her private life. People learned things about Miss Monroe they didn't even dream of knowing about Garbo. If Garbo wanted to flout the rules of the love life in private by looking mannish and suggesting the bachelor rather than the spinster, it was her business; if the "business" was funny, so was that of the Sphinx . . . *in any sane world*. People go love-crazy in a variety of ways—this much is elementary in a day when the Freudian enlightenment has dispelled the mystery of sex by making dream-symbolism a game of alphabet blocks.

There was something rarefied, if not irregular, about Garbo's choices of intimate male friends. One was the health-food advocate Gayelord Hauser; another was Leopold Stokowski. Once she was suspected of hiding away in a house with the latter. These, at any rate, were attachments that could not be suspected as fabrications of a studio, which, as everyone knows, promotes the appearance of love-affairs among its star employees as a matter of good business. Who had *cared* whether she had really been in love with her leading man, John Gilbert? Love is more a routine thing in the civilized world than some moralists are inspired to imagine and maintain. But the tastes of a Gayelord Hauser, the age of the white-locked Stokowski, these looked like things that bore out the private-life legend of Garbo as furnished by newspaper glimpses of her before and after retirement. My point is that all such "eccentricities" are part of the "hard luck" of an illicit love that won't pretend to be anything else. The public at once *envies* the exhibition of all-consuming love and *doubts* that exhibition. It's just too expensive, both to the purse and one's health. Look at what happened to Elizabeth Taylor. Nature gave her a rough time. Of course, it is a fairly egregious fact that she got her man; but not, as many a newspaper reader reminds himself, without paying a considerable forfeit. As to the extent and character of this "forefeit," everyone has a right to his private opinion.

The truth was that in a twinkling, and whether taken humorously or seriously, Garbo's career had collapsed on top of her, and all that was left was the eccentric ex-professional: the low heels, the lanky hair and floppy hat, the perpetual suits, the glimpses of gauntness, the averted face. I shan't quibble. The persistent legend of the *retired* Garbo is a comic one. It couldn't be otherwise in a world as much saturated with tabloid emotions as with radioactivity. The reason one can admit this with any dignity is that Garbo, the Woman of Passion as a "saintly" legend, has survived. She was closer to the truth than she knew when she felt the desire to play St. Francis! Garbo, otherwise, survives as the relic and the defiantly negligent enigma. *Two-Faced Woman*, the career failure, had its obscure point. Garbo's own history had dis-

tinguished between a *private* and a *public* Garbo but her last film had
formulated this duality with the superficiality of a comic-strip drama.

Garbo *lost*. But losing this way is the special privilege of the fabu-
lously successful. Garbo seemed to chuck it and go on her ascetic,
luxuryless, puzzling, private way. Even vulgar reactions to Garbo, today, have their restraint, their quietus, their vague respect. She con-
tributed something to the theatre of romantic passion: a certain sincere
renunciation of it that creates—*still creates*, I would say—the awe pro-
voked whenever a beautiful girl elects to become a nun and hide away
from the world and its sex. Even a film actress or two has gone into
a nunnery, not perhaps without a sincere urge, though the urge may
not have lasted. To have the Garbo genius and renunciation too! *That*
has been reserved for Garbo alone. There are cynics, doubtless, who
put a discreditable construction on her act of retirement, unrepudiated
now for two decades. "She wasn't 'through' . . . etc., etc." Nothing
is easier to guess, anyway; what is difficult, and desirable, is a kind of
certainty.

One recalls how extraordinarily she conveyed boredom, discourage-
ment, a tired irony—exactly by lifting one of those grandly arched
eyebrows. Or simply by letting her wide mouth droop in its own odd
waywardness: observe some of the portraits that follow. Then there was
the quiet, shadowy way she had of smiling with a wince; it was a
smile whose sourness seemed so generous and understanding. These
expressions made her Anna Christie believable past all the imposture
of Garbo being a drab, *Garbo* being the *victim of the male conspiracy!*
Did some humility lurk in this magical bosom—and magically framed
bosom—that was militant, that could not be put down by pride? I
think the fact of the greatest significance that it was repeatedly ru-
mored she would make a comeback in the films as the Duchesse de
Langeais. Balzac's long story, with the name of that heroine as its
title, is about the battle of the sexes: love as aristocratic strength,
pride and independence in two people who, at bottom, cannot resist
each other. Yet they manage to do so—out of sheer pride, out of wanting to be the boss; they do so mutually until, in a crucial twist of irony
in the romantic plot, it is too late.

The Duchess' impassioned opponent is a great Napoleonic soldier,
Montriveau, who has become a General. There are many things sep-
arating them besides sex. The Duchess has a husband. But something
about Montriveau appeals to her and she starts an intricate game of
flirtation, meaning to make mock of his ultimate fall into the trap. It is
the typed Garbo romance. The terrible sex-power of Venus, first successful and then anticlimactically humbled, as when she has to beg
Adonis for his love. After humiliating herself enough to cause a public
scandal as the General's lover, the Duchess hides herself away in a
convent so that Montriveau, with a sudden change of heart, cannot find

her, search as he will; he searches so hard that finally he does discover her, now a nun, and puts through a spectacular plot to kidnap her from the "impregnable" Carmelite convent. But, when he can finally put his hands on her, she is dead. She had really chosen God instead of the human lover who caused her so much suffering. No one would deny the romantic, definitely dated extravagance of this story. But it is no more implausible than the film versions of many of the stories Garbo played in, stories that come back nowadays in revivals.

Excessive passion cancels itself out. This has always been the essence of the romantic theme and its chief moral as illustrated in late fiction and early legend. Only the gods got away unchastened by all-shattering erotic desire, and at times *they* didn't. Garbo stayed human by an obstinate drive to be rid of this thing, *love*, that led to death. She "gave up" love in so many ways that at last she really wanted to *purge* herself of it. Let it go once and for all! But the end could not be achieved, it could only be in sight, if her filmic reincarnations of it should go on and on. "Love" had been her professional authenticity and dignity, the very portrait of her power as an actress—but to hell with it if the catharsis worked only with audiences, not with her!

Whatever the reason, it *didn't* work with her, not with the deep-down her. This is why the ideal role I have always dreamed of for Garbo—so much so that several times I have been on the point of writing her about it—is that of Mademoiselle de Maupin: again a French heroine; again, a heroine giving her name to the story; again, a romance of sensual antithesis; of love, so to speak, at war *with itself*. But this time it is in perfect harmony with the Garbo who, as Queen Christina in one of her films, disguised herself as a man, the Garbo who disliked furbelows and yet had to wear them as "plumage." The Garbo I mean went naked to the truth, and dressing in the severity of a man's clothes is as symbolically naked as any woman who envies the opposite sex its domination can get. Garbo would pretend to be the woman before whom men prostrate themselves. Wanting, very mysteriously, to be the prostrate one, it was the men she envied. To be the woman, denied happiness in love by a turn of fate, was not enough; to be the punished Vampire, the frustrated mistress, was not enough. She wanted to be denied the pleasures of one sex, in the first place, or in the second place, to have the pleasures of both sexes. So it seemed to the "person" inside those heroines with the starlit eyes and the impressionable flesh. . . .

This is not, I think, a very daring thought. It's so obviously a purely romantic thought, and one so impracticable, too. I noted the fine network of small lines about the ends of Garbo's lips when I saw her close and also one fanning from each eye; she even had a set of them, like a sign of neurotically nurtured pride, about the delicate bow of her brief upper lip. Mademoiselle de Maupin was *young*, so young that she could play Shakespeare's Rosalind during the course of the story. The main point about this elegant romance by Théophile Gautier is that the heroine, who masquerades as a cavalier, is a mysteriously bisexual being: a complete, perfect, and beautiful woman who goes about as a man (being able to take to the sword if necessary) because of a moral idea: the female is too vulnerable (vide *Anna Christie*!) and must therefore conceal her vulnerability by habitual masquerade. To add a toothsome sauce of paradox to the dish, Gautier has her traveling about the country with a very young virgin, who is her sister—duly dressed, of course, as a boy.

One can think what one likes. Everybody does, in his own bosom, anyway. Gautier's inspiration was surely due, partly, to the sublime philosophic transvestite, Seraphita, created by Balzac on a mythical mountain-top in Garbo's part of the world. Seraphita is a man to a woman and a woman to a man: a Swedenborgian angel in arbitrary human form. Paradox is a sex, in Seraphita's case, no less than sex a paradox. So the most ancient legends have it. So Plato put it in the mouth of Aristophanes in his Symposium. The original being was hermaphroditic; or rather, in the strictest sense, the original being was asexual, and the two sexes resulted from its being split. Here is the "comic relief" of the other theories of the identity of love as expressed by members of the symposium in Plato's dialogue.

Mademoiselle de Maupin, on the other hand, was molded from a quite different direction as well: Shakespeare's *As You Like It*. Gautier unquestionably bore in mind the piquant fact that in Shakespeare's time the roles of women were taken on the stage by youths. *He* prefers to begin with a maiden and have her sexual identity guessed, when she plays Rosalind at a semi-private performance of *As You Like It*, by a man who is strangely attracted to this fairest of young men, who is really the opposite sex. The paradox is multi-dimensional, all the more so because, in the Gautier story, "Rosalind" herself is supposedly a boy in masquerade; this "boy" then proceeds, as Shakespeare's Rosalind, to disguise "herself" as a boy in order to be near the man she has fallen in love with. This man, then, in the forest of Arden, asks the casually-met, disguised Rosalind, to whom he had mutually been attracted but whom he cannot recognize, to pretend, as a "boy," that he is a girl, so that the young man can practise the love speeches he hopes one day to address to Rosalind. So in the little charade scene that follows, he and Rosalind are really making verbal love to each other, a fact known to her but not to him. Gautier rang a change on this provoking sexual situation by making Mlle. de Maupin's lover guess her true sex because, though outwardly a boy, she plays the part of Rosalind so eloquently.

This kind of fun—I mean Gautier's—is surely extravagant for our day, but not altogether alien. There was *Some Like It Hot*! Yet the

Maupin story, though it ends in a concrete sexual innuendo, is as cool as Garbo in the midst of a scene. Garbo had a way of "letting herself go" according to metered measure. This made for fine craftsmanship in an erotic personality but not high-powered sex to overwhelm the spectator below the waist. In the light of the theatrical innuendo and the exhibition of all varieties of sex, prevalent for the past six or seven years, Garbo playing Maupin would have looked somewhat Victorian. As beautifully complex as her story is, Maupin herself seems the heroine of a Victorian romance gifted with traditional French candor. Anyway, the spark in Garbo, that would have embodied Gautier's heroine, is dead. I did not mean to be so funereal as this when I began. It is merely that thinking about Garbo has taken me to the celebration of the might-have-been. Let me turn back to the legend, which is still alive.

It breathes. Like the real woman, Greta Garbo, it still breathes. That little screening at which we found ourselves was of a film document showing one of the older Kabuki plays, in which traditionally the female roles are taken exclusively by men. There was a very remarkable scene in which the female lead (played by a famous male actor) carries about a severed head as if fondling it, afraid of dropping it, and imbued with pity and terror at having to hold it. There sat Garbo, watching . . . How resplendent seems the art of acting! It is all *impersonation,* whether the sex underneath is true or not. An Elizabeth Taylor may succeed in acting her real self. The legend grows that a Marilyn Monroe does, too, and yet *is* another self, and yearns to act that hidden or possible self. Who seemed more themselves than did Mae West and Marlene Dietrich? But Chaplin's case, alone, shows that a human personality is too complex to be expressed by one character alone; that, as mind and body change and grow, the actor has a desire to play new parts. These stages of change are biological. From the most ancient times the most solemn of rituals, the *rites de passage,* were invented to help people through these stages: there was a mimic death, a mimic rebirth; boy became man, girl became woman; a boy, it is now believed, wore a girl's clothes during the rite because he was being severed from the sex of his mother; so did a girl, wearing a boy's clothes when she was initiated from maidenhood into womanhood.

These are mysteries usually not at all connected with the commonplace image of the Sphinx. But they *are* connected with that image, and with the legend of Oedipus' vanquishing of the Sphinx. For our day, only the fable remains, only the wonder of a strange tragedy, alive for us because repeated in our midst; yes, even by items in the newspapers. Garbo as the Sphinx was a publicity gag, as almost *anything* can be a publicity gag. Even the serious, the polite, and the learned have their "gags." The redoubtable Henry James once charac-

terized George Sand, female novelist, as, if a *lady*, certainly no *gentle-man*. He was taking a sideswipe at the fact that she went around dressed as a man. The wit is jocose and a bit heavy, as James's wit inclined to be when it came to sex. The romance about Mademoiselle de Maupin is sublimely serio-comic. If Garbo had played it, she would have had everything her art could give without seeming to take the religious oath of a nun or a St. Francis. As Anna Karenina she even had a child. So, as a woman (insofar as an actress can be one), there would have been nothing else to have. The truth is, every great actress wants this kind of versatility. Asta Nielsen, Garbo's countrywoman, wanted it, and played Hamlet to get it. Sarah Bernhardt, at a rather advanced age, played the young Napoleon in *L'Aiglon* (*The Eaglet*). Oh, well— I'm beginning to drool. . . . Garbo *is* nice and *was* nice, and drooling never could be nice. So: Farewell, Mademoiselle de Maupin!

The Films of Greta Garbo

Peter the Tramp

An Erik A. Petschler Production (1922)

CAST

   Erik A. Petschler, Greta Gustafsson, Helmer Larsson, Fredrik Olsson, Tyra Ryman, Gucken Cederborg

CREDITS

   Directed and written by Erik A. Petschler.

SYNOPSIS

   Peter (Erik A. Petschler) joins the army after fleeing from the repercussions of a love affair. Greta (Greta Gustafsson) is one of the daughters of a mayor at whose town Peter's army regiment is stationed.

   Peter's escapades include a love affair with Greta, plus an impersonation, and end with his marrying a rich widow.

   This Swedish-made film was Garbo's first feature film. She was billed in the cast under her real name, Greta Gustafsson. This was a comedy, but she was not to make another until *Ninotchka* in 1939.

   The Swedish title of this movie is *Luffar-Petter.*

FACING PAGE: *Greta Garbo as she appeared shortly before her first film was made.*

BELOW: *On location for "Peter the Tramp," with Garbo at extreme left.*

The Story of Gösta Berling

Svensk Filmindustri (1924)

CAST

Lars Hanson, Greta Garbo, Ellen Cederstrom, Mona Martenson, Jenny Hasselquist, Karin Swanstrom, Gerda Lundequist, Torsten Kammeren, Svend Tornbech, Otto Elg Lundberg, Sixten Malmerfelt

CREDITS

Directed by Mauritz Stiller. Adaptation by Mauritz Stiller and Ragnar Hyltén-Cavallius from the novel by Selma Lagerlöf. Photography by Julius Jaenzon.

SYNOPSIS

Gösta Berling (Lars Hanson), a minister, loses his position in the church because of his overindulgence in alcohol. He becomes involved in high society and the women that belong to it.

He meets Countess Dohna (Greta Garbo) and falls in love with her. He sees in her qualities lacking in other women he has known. Eventually, it is she who helps him to redeem himself.

This was a Swedish film and Garbo's second. An edited version under the title *Legend of Gösta Berling* was released in the United States in 1928. It has also been called *Gösta Berling's Saga* and *Atonement of Gösta Berling*.

Director Mauritz Stiller was to help Garbo in her career more than any other person. It was this film that caused L. B. Mayer to bring the two to Hollywood.

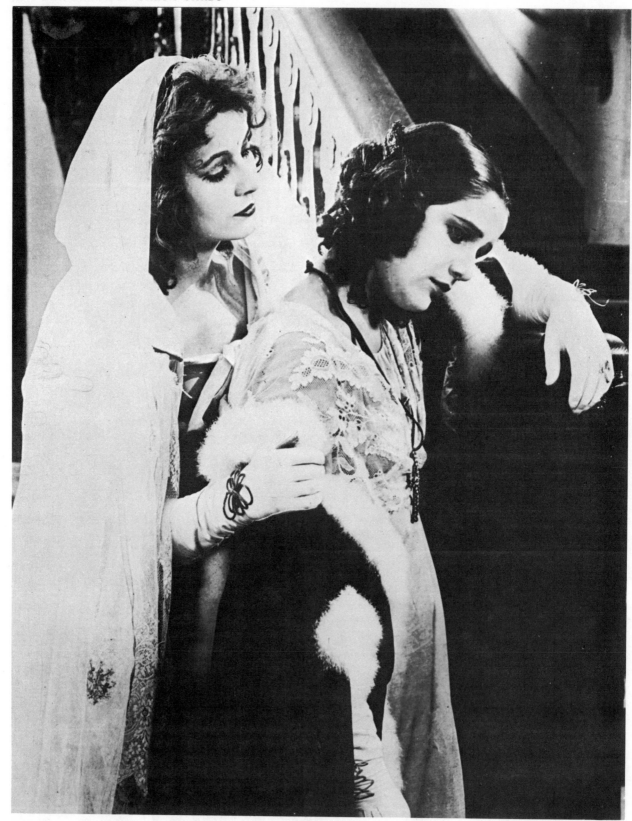

With Mona Mertenson

With Lars Hanson

What the critics said about
THE STORY OF GÖSTA BERLING

Classic Magazine:

Splendid acting and a great woman novelist are the combination that make *The Story of Gösta Berling* far and away the best Swedish picture of the year. Selma Lagerlöf's brilliant novel lends itself well to screen adaptation. It is a period play of the early nineteenth century in Sweden. The quaint costumes of the day have been excellently reproduced, and the charming backgrounds faithfully reconstructed. The carefully balanced and well-selected cast is headed by Jenny Hasselquist, Lars Hanson, and Greta Gustafsson.

Variety:

Interest lies chiefly in the background, foreign locales unfamiliar to this side. Also interesting is the appearance of Greta Garbo, totally unlike the sleeky dame M-G-M's experts made of her. Still a picture only for the sure-seat circle. . . . Story based on what is described as a Nobel Prize novel. Must be another case of a great literary effort lost between the scenario and the cutting room. . . . Clergyman angle led to the Fifth Avenue Playhouse billing the picture as the doings of a "glorified Elmer Gantry."

The Street of Sorrow

A Sofar-Film (1925)

CAST

Werner Krauss, Asta Nielsen, Jaro Furth, Greta Garbo, Agnes Esterhazy, Gregor Chmara, Valeska Gert, Einar Hanson, Loni Nest, Marlene Dietrich

CREDITS

Directed by G. W. Pabst. Adaptation by Willy Haas from the novel by Hugo Bettauer. Photography by Guido Seeber.

SYNOPSIS

Postwar Vienna is filled with greedy men and, opposed to them, families made poor by the war. Franz Rumfort (Jaro Furth) is the head of such an impoverished family. Greta (Greta Garbo) is the eldest of his daughters and is trying to hold the family together.

Maria Lechner (Asta Nielsen) is part of this society. She has a lover, and kills to keep him from marrying someone else. Then she turns herself in to save her lover. A butcher (Werner Krauss), who symbolizes the type of lecher that a postwar society can create, is killed by those he has abused.

Greta is about to become a woman of ill-repute when she is saved by her father, with the help of a Red Cross lieutenant (Einar Hanson).

Garbo's third film, and her only German-made movie. After this, she came to Hollywood to work for Metro-Goldywn-Mayer.

The original German title of this picture was *Die Freudlose Gasse*. It appeared in England under the title *The Joyless Street*. The film also seems to have been shown in this country under that title, but the edited version in general release was called *The Street of Sorrow*.

It is interesting to note that Marlene Dietrich played a minor role in this film.

What the critics said about
THE STREET OF SORROW

Film Daily:

Unsuited for the average audience. Film might originally have been, but the obviously-cut remains make for a badly jumbled picture. Greta Garbo, Asta Nielsen, Einar Hanson and Werner Krauss capable, but their work is greatly overshadowed by the picture's shortcomings. Probably there was a picture here, but the evident mutilation of the censors has left but scattered remnants of a story which gives every indication of having served some high-flung sensations in its original form. . . . The production is poor, the atmosphere drab, and the tempo far too slow.

Variety:

The picture's only commercial value is the presence at the head of the cast of Greta Garbo. . . . It's a lobby asset rather than a screen recommendation, for the role is a poor one, of a rather furtive and bedraggled heroine. . . . A pretty dingy lot are these Vienna daughters of joy. Several elaborate bits are introduced, apparently with the intent to exploit the gay night life of Vienna. It doesn't register gaiety, but rather drab squalor.

FACING PAGE:
With Valeska Gert

RIGHT:
With Jaro Furth

With Werner Krauss

The Torrent

THE TORRENT

A Metro-Goldwyn-Mayer Picture (1926)

CAST

Ricardo Cortez, Greta Garbo, Gertrude Olmstead, Edward Connelly, Lucien Littlefield, Martha Mattox, Lucy Beaumont, Tully Marshall, Mack Swain, Arthur Edmund Carew, Lillian Leighton, Mario Carillo

CREDITS

Directed by Monta Bell. Adaptation by Dorthy Farnum from the novel by Vicente Blasco-Ibáñez. Titles by Katherine Hilliker and H. H. Caldwell. Photography by William Daniels. Edited by Frank Sullivan.

SYNOPSIS

Leonora Moreno (Greta Garbo) and Rafael Brull (Ricardo Cortez) have grown up together in the same Spanish village. Although they are in love, he is from an aristocratic family and dominated by his mother (Martha Mattox).

His mother talks over the matter with Leonora's mother (Lucy Beaumont) and they decide to break up the two lovers. Leonora is sent to Paris, while Rafael becomes engaged to Remedios (Gertrude Olmstead), his mother's choice.

Leonora becomes a famous prima donna and returns to visit her home. She and Rafael meet again and their love is rekindled. His mother separates them again, and he marries Remedios.

Years later, they meet and part. She is still beautiful, but he has become middle-aged. He returns to his wife and family, while Leonora goes on with her career.

This was Garbo's fourth film and her first in Hollywood. M-G-M was to make all her future vehicles. Photographer William Daniels was to be assigned to work on almost all her movies. This was Ricardo Cortez's only role opposite Garbo.

What the critics said about
THE TORRENT

Richard Watts, Jr.
in the *New York Herald Tribune:*

She seems an excellent and attractive actress with a surprising propensity for looking like Carol Dempster, Norma Talmadge, ZaSu Pitts, and Gloria Swanson in turn. That does not mean she lacks a manner of her own, however.

Laurence Reid
in *Motion Picture:*

Probably the most important feature of the film is the latest Greta from Sweden. This is the Greta Garbo, a pretty, wistful, and intensely feminine young person, who suggests a composite picture of a dozen of our best-known stars. Making her debut in the film, she registers a complete success. She is not so much an actress as she is endowed with individuality and magnetism.

Pictures:

In the simplest diction possible, we wish to say that among the many who have been hailed as the "finds" of the year, Greta Garbo stands head of the line, in our opinion. She possesses that which has heretofore only been laid at the door of Pola Negri—fire, animation, abandon and all of the other adjectives usually employed to describe a very colorful figure and personality to match. Moreover Greta has a delightfully youthful figure and a face that is strangely attractive, though not at all beautiful. As the prima donna life gave to and took from as it chose, Miss Garbo, if one can judge by an audience's response, made a very impressive cinema debut in America.

Variety:

Greta Garbo, making her American debut as a screen star, might just as well be hailed right here as the find of the year. This girl has everything, with looks, acting ability, and personality. When one is a Scandinavian and can put over a Latin characterization with sufficient power to make it most convincing, need there be any more said regarding her ability? She makes *Torrent* worth while. . . . There are other "names" in the cast, and, although veterans, they could not overshadow Greta Garbo. Hail this girl, for she'll get over.

ABOVE: *With Ricardo Cortez*
BELOW: *With Lucy Beaumont*

The Temptress

A Metro-Goldwyn-Mayer Picture (1926)

CAST

Greta Garbo, Antonio Moreno, Marc MacDermott, Lionel Barrymore, Armand Kaliz, Roy D'Arcy, Alys Murrell, Steve Clemento, Roy Coulson, Robert Anderson, Francis McDonald, Hector A. Sarno, Virginia Brown Faire, Inez Gomez

CREDITS

Directed by Fred Niblo. Adaptation by Dorothy Farnum from the novel by Vicente Blasco-Ibáñez. Titles by Marion Ainslee. Photography by Tony Gaudio. Edited by Lloyd Nosler.

SYNOPSIS

Elena (Greta Garbo), married to Marquis Fontenoy (Marc MacDermott), is given by her husband to a banker, so that the husband may have money to live in luxury.

At a masquerade, Elena meets Manuel Robledo (Antonio Moreno), an Argentine engineer, and they fall in love. Although she has had several affairs, Manuel is the first man she had really loved.

When he learns she is married, he goes back to Argentina. Elena follows him there. Her husband is killed. Manuel's aides at a dam project fight over her and murder occurs. Manos Duros (Roy D'Arcy), an enemy of Manuel, dynamites the dam. Trying to repair the dam, Manuel's efforts are frustrated by a storm. Manuel blames Elena for all the trouble and goes to kill her. However, he still loves her and Elena leaves, realizing she will bring only ruin to him if she stays.

Years later, Manuel is in Paris with his fiancée, Celinda (Virginia Brown Faire), and discovers that Elena is a streetwalker. Before he departs, he slips money into her purse to help her out.

This, Garbo's fifth film, was the only one in which Antonio Moreno appeared. It also marked the first appearance of Lionel Barrymore with her. The direction of this movie was begun by Mauritz Stiller, Garbo's friend and adviser, but because of difficulties with the studio, Stiller was removed from the assignment and replaced by Fred Niblo.

FACING PAGE:
With Antonio Moreno

With H. B. Warner

With Antonio Moreno

What the critics said about
THE TEMPTRESS

Robert E. Sherwood
in *Life:*

I want to go on record as saying that Greta Garbo in *The Temptress* knocked me for a loop. I had seen Miss Garbo once before, in *The Torrent*, and had been mildly impressed by her visual effectiveness. In *The Temptress*, however, this effectiveness proves positively devastating. She may not be the best actress on the screen—I am powerless to formulate an opinion on her dramatic technique—but there is no room for argument as to the efficacy of her allure. . . . [She] qualifies herewith as the official Dream Princess of the Silent Drama Department of *Life.*

Mordaunt Hall
in the *New York Times:*

Greta Garbo, the accomplished Swedish actress who graced the pictorial translation of Blasco-Ibáñez' *Torrent*, wins new honors at the Capitol in the version of another story by the Spanish author. . . . None of the figurantes in the film appears to be in the least conscious of the camera, and there are moments when Miss Garbo reflects a characteristic mood by the slightest movement of one of her eyelids. . . . Miss Garbo is not only remarkably well suited for the role, but with a minimum of gestures and an unusual restraint in her expressions, she makes every scene in which she appears a telling one. She is attractive and svelte of figure and gives an emphatically effective performance in her impersonation of Elena's heartlessness.

Harriette Underhill
in the *New York Herald Tribune:*

This is the first time we have seen Miss Garbo and she is a delight to the eyes! We may also add that she is a magnetic woman and a finished actress. In fact, she leaves nothing to be desired. Such a profile, such grace, such poise, and most of all, such eyelashes. They swish the air at least a half-inch beyond her languid orbs. Miss Garbo is not a conventional beauty, yet she makes all other beauties seem a little obvious.

Dorothy Herzog
in the *New York Mirror:*

Greta Garbo vitalizes the name part of this picture. She *is* the Temptress. Her tall, swaying figure moves Cleopatra-ishly from delirious Paris to the virile Argentine. Her alluring mouth and volcanic, slumbrous eyes enfire men to such passion that friendships collapse.

Flesh and the Devil

A Metro-Goldwyn-Mayer Picture (1927)

CAST

John Gilbert, Greta Garbo, Lars Hanson, Barbara Kent, William Orlamund, George Fawcett, Eugenie Besserer, Marc MacDermott, Marcelle Corday

CREDITS

Directed by Clarence Brown. Adapted by Benjamin F. Glazer from the novel "The Undying Past" by Hermann Sudermann. Titles by Marion Ainslee. Photography by William Daniels. Edited by Lloyd Nosler.

SYNOPSIS

Leo von Sellenthin (John Gilbert) and Ulrich von Kletzingk (Lars Hanson) have been friends for many years and have estates near each other in Austria.

Leo has been having an affair with Felicitas (Greta Garbo), the wife of Count von Rhaden (Marc MacDermott). The Count learns of this, and Leo kills him in a duel. Leo is forced to leave for America, and Ulrich marries Felicitas, unaware of her affair with Leo.

A few years later, Leo returns when he learns he will not be punished because of the duel. Felicitas again lures him into an affair. When Ulrich finds out, she says that Leo tempted her. Ulrich and Leo have a duel.

Felicitas, not wanting Leo killed, hastens across an ice-packed river to prevent it. She falls through the ice and drowns. Leo wounds Ulrich in the duel, but nurses him back to health and the two become friends again.

This was Garbo's sixth film and her first with John Gilbert. They became a romantic duo both on and off the screen. This film also marked Lars Hanson's first American film appearance with her.

Garbo went on strike for a better salary from M-G-M after *Flesh and the Devil* was completed, and won a better contract.

Barbara Kent, John Gilbert, Greta Garbo, and Lars Hanson

With John Gilbert

With Lars Hanson, Barbara Kent, and John Gilbert

With John Gilbert

What the critics said about
FLESH AND THE DEVIL

Mordaunt Hall
in the *New York Times:*

Produced with admirable artistry, both in the unfurling of the chronicle and in the character delineation, *Flesh and the Devil* . . . is a compelling piece of work in which there are but a few conventional movie notes. . . . Miss Garbo is undeniably alluring as Felicitas.

Photoplay:

Here is the picture filmed when the romance of Jack Gilbert and Greta Garbo was at its height. Naturally, the love scenes (and there are several thousand feet of them) are smoulderingly fervent. . . . Miss Garbo gives a flashing performance of Felicitas, Gilbert is a dashing Leo, although he does overshade some of his scenes, and Lars Hanson is excellent as Ulrich.

Variety:

Here is a picture that is the pay-off when it comes to filming love scenes. There are three in this picture that will make anyone fidget in their seat and their hair rise on end—an' that ain't all. It's a picture with a great kick, a great cast and great direction. . . . Miss Garbo, properly handled and given the right material, will be as great a money asset as Theda Bara was to Fox in years past. This girl has everything.

310-73

Love

A Metro-Goldwyn-Mayer Picture (1927)

CAST

Greta Garbo, John Gilbert, George Fawcett, Emily Fitzroy, Brandon Hurst, Philippe de Lacy

CREDITS

Directed by Edmund Goulding. Adaptation by Frances Marion from the novel "Anna Karenina" by Leo Tolstoy. Titles by Marion Ainslee and Ruth Cummings. Photography by William Daniels. Edited by Hugh Wynn.

SYNOPSIS

Anna Karenina (Greta Garbo) is married to a well-to-do man in Russia during the czarist era. She meets Vronsky (John Gilbert), a military man, and falls in love with him.

Her husband, Karenin (Brandon Hurst), refuses her a divorce, so she leaves him and her child, Seresha (Philippe de Lacy). She becomes Vronsky's mistress.

Vronsky soon wishes to return to his military life. Anna senses that she is losing him. Realizing that she has nothing to go back to and nothing to look forward to after Vronsky goes back to his military calling, Anna throws herself in front of a train at the railroad station.

Garbo's seventh film had John Gilbert opposite her for the second time. It was remade in 1935 and titled *Anna Karenina*, with Frederic March playing the role of Vronsky. Unlike the 1935 version, *Love* was done in modern dress.

With John Gilbert

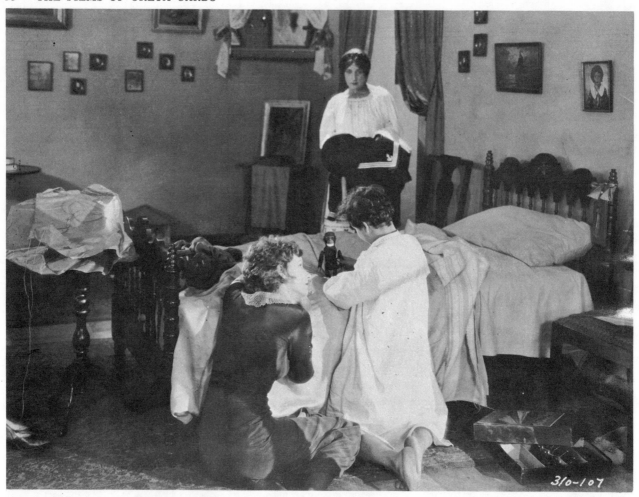

With Emily Fitzroy and Philippe de Lacy

What the critics said about
LOVE

Mordaunt Hall
in the *New York Times:*

 Greta Garbo, the Swedish actress, outshines any
other performance she has given on the screen. Miss
Garbo's singularly fine acting as Anna held the
audience in unusual silence. . . . Miss Garbo is elusive.
Her heavy-lidded eyes, the cold whiteness of her face,
and her svelte figure compel interest in her actions.
Sometimes she reminds one of a blonde Mona Lisa
and on other occasions she is gentle and lovely.
Only in one sequence does she seem to be a little out
of character and that is probably due to obedience
to the director's instructions.

Motion Picture:

 Lovers of Tolstoy will be disappointed. Those who
like to study the Gilbert-Garbo embraces will be
disappointed. In fact, the only people who won't be
disappointed, like myself, are those who have always
thought of Greta Garbo merely as the only woman
in pictures who dresses worse than Alice Terry.
Because Greta is surprising, and her grace and
beauty and fine acting make a cheap, melodramatic

With George Fawcett

picture into something at least interesting, if not good. I recommend it solely that you may see what she was able to do with little help from the script, the director, or John Gilbert.

Variety:

Try and keep the femmes away from this one. They've all apparently got a Gilbert-Garbo complex tucked away somewhere. . . . The girls get a great kick out of the heavy love stuff. They come out of these pictures with their male escorts and an "I wonder-if-he's-learned-anything" expression. They claim the screen's the closest they can get to it. But pity the poor modern lover. He's so tired from holding up a raccoon coat he can't compete, so no wonder there's an aching heart for every clinch in Hollywood. . . . Peculiar combination this Gilbert-Garbo hook-up. Both sprang up suddenly and fast, Miss Garbo from nowhere. The latter isn't now as big as she should be or will be, always remembering it's the stories that count. Neither has she been in enough pictures of late. But if handled, and she will allow herself to be handled, she's the biggest skirt prospect now in pictures. With the start they've got, Miss Garbo and Mr. Gilbert are in a fair way to become the biggest box office mixed team this country has yet known.

With John Gilbert

With Lars Hanson

The Divine Woman

RIGHT: *With Lowell Sherman*
FAR RIGHT: *With Polly Moran*

A Metro-Goldwyn-Mayer Picture (1928)

CAST

Greta Garbo, Lars Hanson, Lowell Sherman, Polly Moran, Dorothy Cumming, John Mack Brown, Cesare Gravina, Paulette Duval, Jean de Briac

CREDITS

Directed by Victor Seastrom. Adaptation by Dorothy Farnum from the play "Starlight" by Gladys Unger. Titles by John Colton. Photography by Oliver Marsh. Edited by Conrad A. Nervig.

SYNOPSIS

Marianne (Greta Garbo), who was placed on a farm by her mother so that the mother might live her gay life in Paris alone, is finally sent for by her and is brought to Paris by one of her mother's lovers, Legrande (Lowell Sherman). When he makes a pass at her, she hits him and flees, thinking he is dead.

She is befriended by a soldier, Lucien (Lars Hanson). He leaves her with a friend, Mme. Pigonier (Polly Moran), a laundress, and goes off with his regiment. One night, Marianne meets Legrande. He is fascinated by her and vows to make her a big stage star. Excited by the prospect of becoming famous, Marianne becomes his mistress.

Lucien returns, a deserter, and is arrested and imprisoned. When he gets out on parole, he goes to see Marianne and denounces her. She, still in love with Lucien, renounces her career, and leaves Legrande. She becomes impoverished, but Lucien finds her and saves her from self-destruction. They reconcile and leave for South America, where he has a small ranch, to start life anew.

Garbo's eighth film was to be her last with Lars Hanson. Her role in this film was patterned on the life of Sarah Bernhardt. The film marked John Mack Brown's first role in a Garbo movie. In the sound era, he was to become a famous Western star.

With Lars Hanson

FACING PAGE: *With Lowell Sherman*

What the critics said about
THE DIVINE WOMAN

Harriette Underhill
in the *New York Herald Tribune:*

We insist that all those who, in their foolishness, have cried, "There is no screen acting—the figures are but puppets, with the director pulling the strings," go to the Capitol Theater and take a look at Greta Garbo and Lars Hanson in *The Divine Woman.* Many who admit that there is acting on the screen have stated that Miss Garbo did not act, however, that she was only a beautiful woman with a strong appeal.

After seeing her play Marianne in this new Metro-Goldwyn picture, no one ever again could say that. In the first place, we are not at all sure that Miss Garbo is beautiful. It seems to be soul, rather than prettiness, which makes her face so attractive, and no one could call Lars Hanson handsome! Still we cannot for the moment think of any two performances as fine as these offered by a Swedish actress and a Swedish actor.

Elizabeth Goldbeck
in *Motion Picture:*

I must be getting inured to Greta Garbo. In this picture she again seemed very lovely indeed. And I think the secret is that, given a part in which she is expected to be something more than a vamp, she is quite a capable girl. She wakes up and has expressions just like other people and is really charming. In fact, I think you will thoroughly enjoy this picture.

Delight Evans
in *Screenland:*

This picture is a huge disappointment, and, although I am trying to bear up, my emotions get the better of me at times; you see, I counted on Greta Garbo. I rooted myself hoarse for her. The most potent personality on the screen—the girl who made Hollywood actresses look like stock company ingenues —the Swedish marvel at emotional massage—she was all of that. And now, just look at *The Divine Woman.* Here is a new Garbo, who flutters, who mugs. This interestingly reserved lady goes completely Hollywood, all at once. It may have been the part. It may have been the direction—but I don't think so. Miss Garbo seems to me to have only one scene in her usual marvelous quiet manner. . . . But for the rest—excuse me! "I go now!"

The Mysterious Lady

With Gustav von Seyffertitz

A Metro-Goldwyn-Mayer Picture (1928)

CAST

Greta Garbo, Conrad Nagel, Gustav von Seyffertitz, Edward Connelly, Albert Pollet, Richard Alexander

CREDITS

Directed by Fred Niblo. Adaptation by Bess Meredyth from the novel "War in the Dark" by Ludwig Wolff. Titles by Marion Ainslee and Ruth Cummings. Photography by William Daniels. Edited by Margaret Booth.

SYNOPSIS

Before the First World War, Tania (Greta Garbo), a Russian spy, has a love affair with Austrian Captain Karl von Heinersdorff (Conrad Nagel) in order to get secret plans that he has in his possession. She falls in love with him, but steals the plans anyway.

Karl is court-martialed and jailed. His uncle (Albert Pollet) helps him to escape, and Karl goes to Russia to find Tania. He does find her and learns she really loves him.

Tania dedicates herself to Karl's cause and double-crosses her spy chief, General Alexandroff (Gustav von Seyffertitz). She gets papers that Alexandroff received from an Austrian traitor and gives them to Karl. When Alexandroff finds out, Tania is forced to shoot him. She and Karl flee from Russia and go to Austria to clear him and to start a new life.

This was Conrad Nagel's first movie with Garbo and the actress' ninth film.

BOTH PAGES: *With Conrad Nagel*

What the critics said about
THE MYSTERIOUS LADY

Life:

She is the dream princess of eternity—the knockout of the ages. . . . Miss Garbo does it all, and does it gorgeously, and for once in her none-too-even career she is supported by an excellent cast, and directed with imagination and sense by Fred Niblo. I recommend *The Mysterious Lady* highly, even to those who don't feel about Greta Garbo quite as I do.

H.D.S.
in the *New York Morning Telegraph:*

This Garbo girl seems to develop just a little more of that intangible "it" with each picture, and the love scenes between her and Nagel are what might be termed burning. There are love scenes by the score, many of which are in close-ups, with the famous La Garbo kiss given full sway as well as full camera focus.

Mordaunt Hall
in the *New York Times:*

None of the actors are able to do much about it, save to wander through and hope for something better next time. Miss Garbo is pretty, but she doesn't make too good a Russian spy.

Betty Colfax
in the *New York Evening Graphic:*

Miss Garbo takes to a close-up like no other star in Hollywood. She overcomes the handicap of an atrocious wardrobe, big feet, and widening hips with a facility of expression and a charm which still keep her in a class by herself.

FACING PAGE: *With Gustav von Seyffertitz*

With Conrad Nagel

-58

A Woman of Affairs

ABOVE:
*With John Gilbert
and others*

FACING PAGE:
With Lewis Stone

A Metro-Goldwyn-Mayer Picture (1929)

CAST

Greta Garbo, John Gilbert, Lewis Stone, John Mack Brown, Douglas Fairbanks, Jr., Hobart Bosworth, Dorothy Sebastian

CREDITS

Directed by Clarence Brown. Adaptation by Bess Meredyth from the novel "The Green Hat" by Michael Arlen. Photography by William Daniels. Edited by Hugh Wynn.

SYNOPSIS

Diana Merrick (Greta Garbo), an aristocratic English girl, is in love with Neville (John Gilbert). However, his father, Sir Montague (Hobart Bosworth), stops their marriage, because he disapproves of her family's reckless way of life. Her brother, Geoffrey (Douglas Fairbanks, Jr.), is a wastrel, and Diana's own conduct is not beyond reproach.

She begins a series of escapades and winds up marrying David (John Mack Brown), unaware that he is a thief. When David is caught, he commits suicide, and Diana sets out to pay back what he had stolen.

Neville is married to Constance (Dorothy Sebastian), but still loving Diana, he leaves Constance to come back to her. Diana, realizing that their love will ruin him, tells him that his wife is pregnant and sends him away. Then she crashes her car into the tree where she and Neville first discovered they were in love, and dies.

A Woman of Affairs was Garbo's tenth film and her third opposite John Gilbert. It marked Lewis Stone's first part in a Garbo movie. In it, he played a good friend to Diana.

With John Mack Brown

With Lewis Stone and Douglas Fairbanks, Jr.

With John Gilbert

What. the critics said about
A WOMAN OF AFFAIRS

Pare Lorentz
in *Judge:*

The most interesting feature of *A Woman of Affairs* is the treatment accorded it by the censors. As is obvious, the story was adapted from Michael Arlen's best seller, *The Green Hat*, and, as every reader of that Hispano-Suiza advertisement will recollect, the heroine's white feather was borne for the proud fact that her suicide husband suffered from an ailment enjoyed by some of our most popular kings, prelates and prize-fighters. Well, sir, Bishop Hays changes that to "embezzlement." And, for some strange reason, instead of using the word "purity" (the boy died for purity, according to Iris March) they substituted the oft-repeated word "decency." To anyone who can show me why "purity" is a more immoral word than "decency," I'll gladly send an eighty-five cent Paramount ticket, to be used at your own risk. Outside of its purification, the movie is a good dramatization of the novel and for the first time I respected the performance of Greta Garbo. She shuffled through the long, melancholy and sometimes beautiful scenes with more grace and sincerity than I have ever before observed, and the fact that she rode down and practically eliminated John Gilbert's goggling is in itself grounds for recommendation. Another indifferent performer, Douglas Fairbanks, Jr., suddenly snapped to life under the guidance of Director Brown, and gave a splendid performance. Lewis Stone made his usual calm and reserved appearance and, even with its melancholy apathy, you will find *A Woman of Affairs* worth seeing.

Variety:

A sensational array of screen names, and the intriguing nature of the story (*The Green Hat*) from which it was made, together with some magnificence in the acting by Greta Garbo, by long odds the best thing she has ever done, will carry through this vague and sterilized version of Michael Arlen's exotic play. . . . But the kick is out of the material, and, worse yet, John Gilbert, idol of the flappers, has an utterly blah role. Most of the footage he just stands around, rather sheepishly, in fact, while others shape the events. At this performance (the second of the Saturday opening), whole groups of women customers audibly expressed their discontent with the proceedings. . . . Miss Garbo saves an unfortunate situation throughout by a subtle something in her playing that suggests just the exotic note that is essential to the whole theme and story. Without her eloquent acting the picture would go to pieces.

A Metro-Goldwyn-Mayer Picture (1929)

CAST

Greta Garbo, Lewis Stone, Nils Asther

Wild Orchids

CREDITS

Directed by Sidney Franklin. Adaptation by Willis Goldbeck from the story "Heat" by John Colton. Continuity by Hans Kraly and Richard Schayer. Titles by Marion Ainslee. Photography by William Daniels. Edited by Conrad Nervig.

SYNOPSIS

John Sterling (Lewis Stone) takes his young wife Lillie (Greta Garbo) with him when he goes to inspect plantations in the Orient. On shipboard, they meet Prince De Gace (Nils Asther), a Javanese, who becomes interested in Lillie.

When they arrive at their common destination, he entertains the couple at his palace. While Sterling goes about his work, the lonely Lillie accepts the advances of the Prince. Sterling spots them and later finds Lillie's necklace on the couch where she and the Prince were making love.

When the three go on a tiger hunt, Lillie finds her necklace in Sterling's coat and realizes he knows the truth. The two men have gone to hunt down a tiger and she runs to find them suspecting the worst. The Prince discovers his rifle is not loaded and he is attacked by a tiger. Sterling kills the tiger, but the Prince has been badly hurt.

Later, Sterling tells the Prince that he will give Lillie a divorce so that she may be happy. As Sterling prepares to leave for home, he discovers Lillie waiting for him. Lillie tells Sterling that she loves him and they are reconciled.

In this, Garbo's eleventh film, only the three mentioned stars received cast credit. It was Asther's first with Garbo and Stone's second.

ABOVE AND LEFT:
With Nils Asther

FACING PAGE:
With Lewis Stone

What the critics said about
WILD ORCHIDS

Richard Watts, Jr.
in the *New York Herald Tribune:*

As ever, Miss Garbo is not only an alluring personage and a beautiful woman, but likewise an expert actress.

Mordaunt Hall
in the *New York Times:*

Miss Garbo's acting is well-timed and, as usual, effective. It is not an easy role, but she succeeds in imparting to it no small amount of subtlety.

With John Mack Brown (at left)

FACING PAGE: *With Nils Asther*

The Single Standard

A Metro-Goldwyn-Mayer Picture (1929)

CAST

Greta Garbo, Nils Asther, John Mack Brown, Dorothy Sebastian, Lane Chandler, Robert Castle, Mahlon Hamilton, Kathlyn Williams, Zeffie Tilbury

CREDITS

Directed by John S. Robertson. Adaptation by Josephine Lovett from the novel by Adela Rogers St. John. Titles by Marion Ainslee. Photography by Oliver Marsh. Edited by Blanche Sewell.

SYNOPSIS

Arden Stuart (Greta Garbo), a San Francisco debutante, meets Packy Cannon (Nils Asther), a sailor-fighter turned artist, in an art gallery. She falls in love with him and goes off with him on a yacht for a prolonged affair.

When he leaves her to go to Paris on business, she returns to San Francisco and finds herself an outcast. However, Tommy Hewlett (John Mack Brown), who has always loved her, marries her, and they have a child.

Packy returns, and Arden is again attracted to him, causing her husband to contemplate suicide. Arden realizes that her husband and child are more important to her than a romantic escapade, and Packy goes out of her life forever.

This was Garbo's twelfth film and the last with Nils Asther and John Mack Brown.

With John Mack Brown

FACING PAGE: *With Nils Asther and Kathlyn Williams*

What the critics said about
THE SINGLE STANDARD

Pare Lorentz
in *Judge:*

For the first time since she hit these shores, grim Greta Garbo has done a good piece of work. In *The Single Standard* she actually walks, smiles, and acts. I have never been able to understand the universal palpitation that has followed her slow but stupid appearance on the great American screen—sex appeal, unfortunately, is a matter of opinion. Nice legs and much hair might be "it," but it doesn't make an actress. Nevertheless the lady can, and does, act in her latest movie, and the fact that she is homely and awkward while so engaged only make me like her more. However, I'm funny that way—unless a person has a broken nose, a cauliflower ear, or folding ankles, I can never really get interested.

There is not much of a story to *The Single Standard*, although it starts out with a great big bold statement to the effect that if men can, so can women, and the action boils down to the situation wherein a woman is given the choice of leaving her husband and child for an erstwhile free-lance lover or staying with her husband and letting the little one have a respectable woman for a mother. The situation is neatly turned, Miss Garbo works hard and effectively, and on the whole it all furnishes good summer entertainment. The best thing about *The Single Standard* is its muteness.

Variety:

What some girls do today, and a lot more would like to, Greta Garbo does in *The Single Standard*. . . . This, with all of the quickie material and rough story edges, as well as much too blasé Miss Garbo, the thinking buyers will discover shortly after the production gets under way. But the thousands of typing girlies and purple-suited office boys will find this made to their order. Although the lettering in the film would set forth Miss Garbo, as Arden Stuart, throwing off the cloak of conventionalism for free plunges claimed so common in spots here and on the Continent, the actress is most unfeline in her brazen directness. While censors probably expect to leap on this point, when the picture gets to them, they will find no show, except a veiled peep at Arden's garters. The star keeps well wrapped throughout, and her intimate postures are so frequent and so matter of fact after the first dozen times that only once, when expectation is aroused with the initial fall, do they come anywhere near getting an actual kick.

The Kiss

A Metro-Goldwyn-Mayer Picture (1929)

CAST

Greta Garbo, Conrad Nagel, Anders Randolf, Holmes Herbert, Lew Ayres, George Davis

CREDITS

Directed by Jacques Feyder. Adaptation by Hans Kraly from a story by George M. Saville. Photography by William Daniels. Edited by Ben Lewis.

SYNOPSIS

Irene Guarry (Greta Garbo) is the wife of a silk merchant in Lyon. Her husband's partner, Lassalle (Holmes Herbert), has a son, Pierre (Lew Ayres), who is in love with Irene. She resists Pierre's advances, but her husband (Anders Randolf), in a fit of jealousy, tries to kill Pierre. To save the young man, Irene kills her husband with his own gun. Lassale makes Pierre keep silent about the matter.

Irene is brought to trial and André (Conrad Nagel), a lawyer and once her lover, defends her. Lassalle claims Guarry was despondent over business. Irene is acquitted of the charge. She goes off with André, but it remains for her to tell him the true circumstances surrounding her husband's death.

The Kiss was Garbo's second and last film with Conrad Nagel. It was her thirteenth movie and her last silent one.

With Lew Ayres

With Lew Ayres

What the critics said about
THE KISS

Pare Lorentz
in *Judge:*

Greta Garbo and Clara Bow appeared this week in *The Kiss* and *The Saturday Night Kid*, respectively. Miss Garbo is still the wronged but pure lady of passion and Miss Bow, I presume, is still Miss Bow. I don't know that I can add anything to what has already been said.

Motion Picture:

The last stand of the silent pictures, the last hope of those who like 'em quiet is Greta Garbo. Once again she plays one of those mysterious women whose heart no man quite knows, neither her husband nor her lover. A new juvenile, Lew Ayres, plays the infatuated youth so well that one is almost embarrassed at watching his display of adolescent passion. The question of Miss Garbo's appeal is still unsolved by this picture. In spite of unworthy stories, in spite of her stubborn silence in this talkie day, I would gladly pay for my own ticket to see a Garbo picture—which is the greatest compliment a reviewer can pay!

Screenland:

The Swedish charmer carries this load of a mediocre story on her splendid shoulders and so makes *The Kiss* worth seeing. . . . Next to Greta, the most interesting thing about *The Kiss* is the film debut of young Lew Ayres, a smouldering boy who is a real find.

With Conrad Nagel

With George F. Marion

FACING PAGE: *With Marie Dressler*

Anna Christie

A Metro-Goldwyn-Mayer Picture (1930)

CAST

Greta Garbo, Charles Bickford, George F. Marion, Marie Dressler, James T. Mack, Lee Phelps

CREDITS

Directed by Clarence Brown. Adaptation by Frances Marion from the play by Eugene O'Neill. Photography by William Daniels. Edited by Hugh Wynn.

SYNOPSIS

Anna Christie (Greta Garbo) had been left by her sailor father on a farm owned by relatives. She fled from the cruel family and went on her own, eventually becoming a prostitute.

Disgusted with her life and broke, she comes to her father, Chris (George F. Marion), and goes to live on his fishing barge. She meets Marthy (Marie Dressler), an old waterfront woman, who was her father's mistress.

One day, during a storm, they save a seaman named Matt Burke (Charles Bickford) from drowning. Anna and Matt fall in love. However, Anna's anger at her father for neglecting her for so many years causes her to blurt out her past to her father and Matt.

Matt, in disgust, walks out. Unable to stop loving Anna and knowing that he also had made mistakes, Matt returns. He asks Anna to marry him and she accepts.

Anna Christie was Garbo's fourteenth film and her first with sound. It was her only picture with the other three principal cast members.

With Charles Bickford and George F. Marion

With Marie Dressler and Charles Bickford

With George F. Marion and Charles Bickford

With George F. Marion

What the critics said about
ANNA CHRISTIE

Richard Watts, Jr.
in the *New York Herald Tribune:*

Her voice is revealed as a deep, husky, throaty contralto that possesses every bit of that fabulous poetic glamour that has made this distant Swedish lady the outstanding actress of the motion picture world.

Norbert Lusk
in *Picture Play:*

The voice that shook the world! It's Greta Garbo's, of course, and for the life of me I can't decide whether it's baritone or bass. She makes it heard for the first time on the screen in *Anna Christie*, and there isn't another like it. Disturbing, incongruous, its individuality is so pronounced that it would belong to no one less strongly individual than Garbo herself. Yet it doesn't wholly belong to her, but seems a trick of the microphone in exaggerating what in real life probably is merely a low-keyed voice, slightly husky. . . . In choosing *Anna Christie* for her audible debut, the Swedish star attempts one of the most difficult roles in the contemporary theater. The part is almost a monologue, a test for an actress experienced in speech, a brave feat for one who is not. And Garbo makes a magnificent effort, a gallant fight against great odds. She emerges not quite victorious, but crowned with laurels, nevertheless, for her courage. For she can do no wrong.

Mordaunt Hall
in the *New York Times:*

The tall Swedish actress's portrayal of the title role of *Anna Christie* is one that is very true to life. Miss Garbo, being of the same nationality as Anna, gives an enlightening conception of the character. Whether she is dealing with straight English or the vernacular, she compels attention by her deep-toned enunciation and the facility with which she handles Anna's slang. . . .

One soon becomes accustomed to Miss Garbo's surprisingly low intonations. She is a real Anna, who at once enlists sympathy for her hard life. The words and expressions of this girl make one think of her in character, and cause one almost to forget that she is Miss Garbo, the Iris March of the pictorial version of *The Green Hat*, which was known on the screen as *A Woman of Affairs;* the unfortunate woman of *The Kiss;* the Felicitas of *Flesh and the Devil,* and a number of other impersonations. Here she is a Swedish girl to whom life has been anything but kind and who for that reason at the age of thirty is bitterly cynical. . . . All this is splendidly acted by Miss Garbo who proves here that she can handle a forceful role with little or no relief in its dull atmosphere just as well as she can play the part of the fashionably dressed, romantic wife of a moneyed lawyer.

BOTH PAGES: *With Gavin Gordon*

Romance

A Metro-Goldwyn-Mayer Picture (1930)

CAST

Greta Garbo, Lewis Stone, Gavin Gordon, Elliott Nugent, Florence Lake, Clara Blandick, Henry Armetta, Mathilde Comont, Countess De Liguoro

CREDITS

Directed by Clarence Brown. Dialogue and continuity by Bess Meredyth and Edwin Justus Mayer from the play by Edward Sheldon. Photography by William Daniels. Edited by Hugh Wynn and Leslie F. Wilder.

SYNOPSIS

Harry (Elliott Nugent), the grandson of a bishop, (Gavin Gordon) wants to marry an actress. When the bishop learns of this, he tries to dissuade him by relating a part of his own life when he was still Rector Tom Armstrong.

The bishop says that he met a prima donna named Rita Cavallini (Greta Garbo) and fell in love with her. She fell in love with him also and finally confessed that until she met Armstrong she had been the mistress of wealthy Cornelius Van Tuyl (Lewis Stone). After her final performance, Van Tuyl tried to get her to return to him, but she refused. When Armstrong learned that she had seen Van Tuyl, he came to her and denounced her. Then he pleaded with her to spend her last night with him. She begged him not to treat her as other men had, and began praying. Armstrong came to his senses and left. He never saw her again.

His story, however, does not change Harry's mind about marrying an actress. Later, Armstrong reads of Rita's death in a newspaper.

Garbo's fifteenth film marked Lewis Stone's third appearance with her. This was Gavin Gordon's only lead with Garbo.

What the critics said about
ROMANCE

Mordaunt Hall
in the *New York Times:*

Although Greta Garbo's performance in *Romance*
is perhaps as good as anything she has done on the
screen, it would have made the picture far more
credible had the producers seen fit to recognize that
she is no Italian soprano. . . . Miss Garbo, in this
her second talking film, appears to be quite as much
at her ease in speaking her lines as she was in her
old silent picture performances. She is a breath of
life in this love story, which, old as it may be in
theme, really is no more old than love itself. . . . Her
fascinating countenance and her graceful movements
are admirably suited to the role in this slender
narrative which moves along so easily that there is
never an instant one would take one's eyes from
the screen.

Norbert Lusk
in *Picture Play:*

Hollywood's favorite adjective "marvelous" is the
word that first comes to mind on viewing Greta
Garbo in *Romance.* Her performance is a thing
of pure beauty, an inspiring blend of intellect and
emotion, a tender, poignant, poetic portrait of
a woman who thrusts love from her because she
considers herself unworthy of the man who offers
it. Since no mention of Miss Garbo can be made
without reference to her voice, it is a simple matter
to dispose of it at the outset. It is the same voice
that was heard in *Anna Christie,* but it is better
suited to the present role, because the character has
many moods and none of the bitterness of Anna. Rita
Cavallini, the Italian prima donna, is mercurial,
bantering, tender, wistful. What matter if Garbo's
accent only occasionally suggests the Italian's efforts
to speak English? The Garbo voice itself is not of
Italian quality or inflection, but for all any one cares
Rita Cavallini might as well be Portuguese or
Roumanian, for it is her emotions that are conveyed
by Garbo to the spectator, and her nativity counts
for nothing at all. What matter, too, if the picture
as a whole is slow, even draggy, and lacks climaxes?
It is nevertheless absorbing because of Garbo—her
inescapable magnetism, her sure intelligence, her
clear, unflagging talent for communicating to the
spectator her every thought and feeling.

With Lewis Stone

With Gavin Gordon

Inspiration

A Metro-Goldwyn-Mayer Picture (1931)

CAST

Greta Garbo, Robert Montgomery, Lewis Stone, Marjorie Rambeau, Judith Vosselli, Beryl Mercer, John Miljan, Edwin Maxwell, Oscar Apfel, Joan Marsh, Zelda Sears, Karen Morley, Gwen Lee, Paul McAllister, Arthur Hoyt, Richard Tucker

CREDITS

Directed by Clarence Brown. Story and screen play by Gene Markey. Photography by William Daniels. Edited by Conrad A. Nervig.

SYNOPSIS

An artist's model, Yvonne (Greta Garbo), falls in love with André (Robert Montgomery), who is studying for consular service. They become lovers, but he is unaware of her former lovers. When he finds out, he leaves her.

Later, finding her poverty-stricken, he buys a country place for her. When he tells her that he is to marry another, she pleads with him. Reading of the suicide of one of her friends, Liane (Karen Morley), who killed herself when her lover, Delval (Lewis Stone), left her, André determines to forsake his career for her.

He comes to tell Yvonne this and finds one of her former lovers pleading with her to return to him. André says he will forget everything, but when he falls asleep, she writes him a farewell note and leaves, determined not to ruin his life.

Inspiration was Garbo's sixteenth film, and her fourth with Lewis Stone. It was the only film in which Robert Montgomery played opposite Garbo.

With Robert Montgomery

With Robert Montgomery

What the critics said about
INSPIRATION

Mordaunt Hall
in the *New York Times:*

Miss Garbo, no matter what may be said of the story, gives a stunning performance as the girl who is the toast of Paris studios. . . . Miss Garbo endeavors to symbolize Yvonne's mood by different styles of coiffure. In the initial scenes her hair is fluffed up at the sides, and subsequently it has a more subdued aspect. She wears some striking costumes and is virtually the sole subject of interest in this production.

Motion Picture:

When Garbo loves she loves like nobody's business. In *Inspiration* she loves Robert Montgomery to the extent that she is willing to sacrifice her own happiness and her own future to let him have his childhood sweetheart. The ending is *Camille* without the cough.

Variety:

Miss Garbo has never looked or played better than in this picture, a suitable assignment. Replete with heavy love stuff, she plays it easily and convincingly, even contributing a sparkling brief bit of light comedy and often helping long passages of awkward dialogue to sound almost real.

Norbert Lusk
in *Picture Play:*

Handicapped by the material provided for her, Greta Garbo still shines with such brightness that it is only when the picture is well under way that one realizes the weight and dreariness of her burden. For not even the greatest artist maintains effulgence in the murk of a poor picture. That is why laurels for Garbo should be dewed with tears of regret. She makes her heroine sensitive, intelligent, alluring, with a shimmer of laughter like sunshine after an April shower. So superior indeed is Yvonne to the trite circumstances of her story that you feel the player, aware of the disparity, is spurred to greater effort.

With Lewis Stone

With Beryl Mercer

Susan Lenox: Her Fall and Rise

A Metro-Goldwyn-Mayer Picture (1931)

CAST

Greta Garbo, Clark Gable, Jean Hersholt, John Miljan, Alan Hale, Hale Hamilton, Hilda Vaughn, Russell Simpson, Cecil Cunningham, Theodore von Eltz, Marjorie King, Helene Millard, Ian Keith

CREDITS

Directed by Robert Z. Leonard. Adaptation by Wanda Tuchock from the novel by David Graham Phillips. Dialogue by Zelda Sears and Edith Fitzgerald. Photography by William Daniels. Edited by Margaret Booth.

SYNOPSIS

A farmer named Ohlin (Jean Hersholt) wants to marry off his illegitimate daughter, Helga (Greta Garbo), to a brutish man, Mondstrum (Alan Hale). She flees and comes upon a mountain cabin belonging to a construction engineer, Rodney Spencer (Clark Gable). He promises to help her, and they eventually fall in love. When he leaves on business, promising to return and marry her, she learns Ohlin is searching for her. She leaves the cabin and has to take a carnival train to escape.

She has an affair with the owner, Burlington (John Miljan), in order to stay with the carnival. Rodney returns, learns of her affair, and walks out on her, despite her pleas. She becomes the mistress of a wealthy politician, Mike Kelly (Hale Hamilton), and invites Rodney to visit her. She now calls herself Susan Lenox.

He again rejects her, but loving him she sets out to find him. She finds him in South America, a downtrodden man working at a jungle construction camp. He refuses to believe that she has altered her way of life. She almost agrees to go away with a rich man, Robert Lane (Ian Keith), but instead seeks out Rodney again. They are reconciled and begin a new life together.

This was Garbo's seventeenth film, the only one with Gable.

With Alan Hale

With Clark Gable

What the critics said about
SUSAN LENOX: HER FALL AND RISE

Mordaunt Hall
in the *New York Times:*

Being an accomplished actress, Greta Garbo makes the most of a bad bargain in the picturization of David Graham Phillips's novel. . . . Any picture to which Miss Garbo lends her presence is worthy of attention; but, even so, it is rather disappointing to find her in a production which is directed along the lines of old silent film techniques, with halting and often crudely written dialogue and poorly developed episodes.

Never once since she appeared in her first Hollywood film, Ibáñez's *The Torrent*, has she given anything but an excellent account of herself. It is therefore a pity that she does not have better luck with her stories.

Photoplay:

If you like your romance spread thick, your passion strong, and your Garbo hot, don't miss this. And take notice, you Garboites! If you were mad about her before, just wait until you see her teamed up with this manifestation of masculine S.A. called Clark Gable.

Variety:

The picture provides Miss Garbo with a role of a destiny-hounded woman not altogether unlike her Anna Christie and adds to the Garbo gallery another impressive portrait. . . . Once more she achieves an acting effect by means that baffle while they provoke interest. Teaming with the great Garbo, of course, marks the peak of Gable's vogue.

With Clark Gable

With Hale Hamilton and Clark Gable

Mata Hari

A Metro-Goldwyn-Mayer Picture (1932)

CAST

*Greta Garbo, Ramon Novarro, Lionel Barrymore, Lewis Stone,
C. Henry Gordon, Karen Morley, Alec B. Francis, Blanche Frederici,
Edmund Breese, Helen Jerome Eddy, Frank Reicher*

CREDITS

*Directed by George Fitzmaurice. Original story and screen play by
Benjamin Glazer and Leo Birinski. Dialogue by Doris Anderson and
Gilbert Emery. Photography by William Daniels. Edited by Frank
Sullivan.*

SYNOPSIS

Mata Hari (Greta Garbo) is a German spy posing as a dancer in Paris.
She is sent by Andriani (Lewis Stone) to get Russian messages about
military movements needed by the Allies during the First World War.

She meets Lt. Alexis Rosanoff (Ramon Novarro) and has an affair
with him, unaware that he has the messages. General Shubin (Lionel
Barrymore) has been her lover and has passed to her many important
messages in return for her favors. When she learns Rosanoff has the
messages, she spends the night with him, while her fellow agents copy
the messages he has.

When Shubin learns of her affair with Rosanoff, he picks up a phone
and threatens to turn her in as a spy, and Rosanoff too. She shoots
Shubin and makes Rosanoff leave when he looks for the General.

Rosanoff flies back toward Russia and is shot down. She learns he is in
a hospital, blinded, and comes to tell him she still loves him. One of
Andriani's men is sent to kill her for disobeying orders, but he is caught
when she asks a policeman for help. She is finally arrested, however,
and brought to trial.

When Rosanoff is to be called in to testify, she pleads guilty rather
than have him know about her past. Rosanoff is brought to her in jail
thinking she is in a hospital. After their short reunion, she is taken from
her cell and executed by a firing squad.

Mata Hari was Garbo's eighteenth film, and the only one with Novarro.
It was Lionel Barrymore's second and Lewis Stone's fifth with her.

With Lionel Barrymore

With Ramon Novarro

What the critics said about
MATA HARI

Mordaunt Hall
in the *New York Times:*

Changed though it may be from the actual career of Mata Hari, the Dutch dancer and spy, the picture that bears her name is an entertainment of no mean value in which that mysterious actress, Greta Garbo, gives another flawless portrayal. . . . Miss Garbo may not be any more like Mata Hari, whose real name was Margaret Zella MacLeod, than the film narrative is like an authentic account of the spy's career. There is, however, in the skillfully arranged series of incidents enough truth to make a most compelling melodrama.

Variety:

Though Garbo is sexy and hot in a less subtle way this time, and though the plot goes about as far as it can in situation warmth, the story presents nothing sensational. . . . [Garbo] does a polite cooch to Oriental music as a starter, and in the same number makes a symbolic play for a huge idol, with the hips in motion all the while. The finish is a neatly masked strip, with Greta's back to the lens. . . . Two other torrid moments later in the running are given to Garbo and Novarro. Both times they turn out the lights.

Screen Book:

As the German spy, Mata Hari, who wrecked men's lives to gain information, she has the best role of her career·and sets a standard which is almost untouchable. The real Mata Hari was a colorful person, but she could in no way touch the personality displayed by the Swedish star.

With Ramon Novarro

Grand Hotel

A Metro-Goldwyn-Mayer Picture (1932)

CAST

Greta Garbo, John Barrymore, Joan Crawford, Wallace Beery, Lionel Barrymore, Lewis Stone, Jean Hersholt, Robert McWade, Purnell B. Pratt, Ferdinand Gottschalk, Rafaela Ottiano, Morgan Wallace, Tully Marshall, Frank Conroy, Murray Kinnell, Edwin Maxwell

CREDITS

Directed by Edmund Goulding. Adapted by William A. Drake from the play by Vicki Baum. Photography by William Daniels. Edited by Blanche Sewell.

SYNOPSIS

Grusinskaya (Greta Garbo) comes to stay at the Grand Hotel in Berlin. A famous ballet star, she is to perform at a theatre in the city. Baron von Gaigern (John Barrymore), an adventurer, has come to the hotel to steal her jewels.

After a performance, Grusinskaya returns to her apartment, dejected about her career. The Baron is there, but hides when she enters. Seeing that she is contemplating suicide, he reveals himself and claims he has come there because he is an ardent admirer. Eventually, they fall in love.

Also at the hotel is Kringelein, a bookkeeper, who has an incurable disease and plans to enjoy his last moments on earth. He falls in love with Flaemmchen (Joan Crawford), a stenographer, but she desires wealth.

Preysing (Wallace Beery), an industrialist, has come to the hotel to negotiate a business deal which backfires. He is attracted to Flaemmchen and she, wanting money, agrees to have an affair with him.

The Baron, meanwhile, has told Grusinskaya that he will meet her elsewhere after she departs from the hotel and they can start a life together. Needing money, he attempts to rob Preysing's apartment. Preysing catches and kills the Baron.

Kringelein keeps Flaemmchen out of the way when Preysing is arrested. Flaemmchen agrees to go away with Kringelein to spend the rest of his days traveling with him. They both hope someone, somewhere, has a cure for his disease.

Grusinskaya departs with her staff from the hotel, happily planning her new life with the Baron, unaware that he is dead.

Grand Hotel was Garbo's nineteenth film and had the strongest cast of all her pictures. She was not to appear with John Barrymore, Crawford, or Beery again. This film marked Lionel Barrymore's third and Lewis Stone's sixth appearance with Garbo.

With John Barrymore

With John Barrymore

What the critics said about
GRAND HOTEL

John Mosher
in *The New Yorker:*

In spite of the brevity of her appearance, against what many a star would call ground odds, Garbo dominates the picture entirely, making the other players merely competent performers, in my opinion; giving the tricky, clever film a lift, a spring, such as pictures without her, without that intense, nervous vitality she's got, cannot possess.

Percy Hammond
in the *New York Herald Tribune:*

When, not long ago, I questioned the infallibility of Miss Greta Garbo's deportment in *Grand Hotel*, I was unaware of the passionate esteem in which she is held by the film-lovers. Of course, it was known that, like many of her sisterhood, she was enshrined as something holy, sanctifying the places of her performance with the perfumed incenses of her Art. But it was not suspected that she was guarded by a numerous garrison of warlike knights and ladies sworn to shield her from agnostic assaults and batteries. I thought that one could speak of her with the same impudent freedom that one enjoys when disparaging the work of artists of the human drama, without fear of reprisals. No impression, however, could have been more erroneous. Since the publication of my doubts I have been peppered with so many angry letters that I am tempted never again to come within the measure of the screen-fan's wrath. To fellow foreigners intruding on cinema criticism the advice is hereby given, that if they don't like Miss Garbo they'd better go back where they came from. "When in a strange land worship the gods of the place, whatever they are."

Vicki Baum,
author of *Grand Hotel,*
in *Modern Screen:*

If I say that Greta Garbo as the dancer is much better than I expected, that's not of small consequence. For I expected the utmost. I expected that she'd be Greta Garbo and that would have been enough! But this time she did more than usual. She played, so to speak, two roles. First, the weary, lonely dancer, aching for success—and then the awakened woman experiencing a great love. I've always maintained that the ability to transform one's self constitutes great acting. . . . In *Grand Hotel* it's quite different. There were five main roles—the characters were there first and then came the actors—and I'm afraid that not a single one of the big stars viewed his part with much pleasure at first. Here Greta Garbo has achieved something which few people expected of her. She has fitted herself into a play and into a cast and has rendered a great performance exactly at that point where the role was contrary to her own being. The twittering, laughing, hopping about, in the tarlatan of a ballet skirt is certainly not what Greta would have sought out as her role. But she has accomplished it. She's gone the whole way which led from her first words, "I have never been so tired in my life," to the last words, "It will be sunny in Tramezzo. We'll have a guest, Suzette." That dead-tired face in the beginning—where did Greta get those small sad lines around her mouth and forehead? Then, that face in which—between laughter and tears—love awakens! That face full of wanton joy when she is happy. That face full of fear when she waits for her beloved in vain. Unforgettable! Thank you, Greta Garbo.

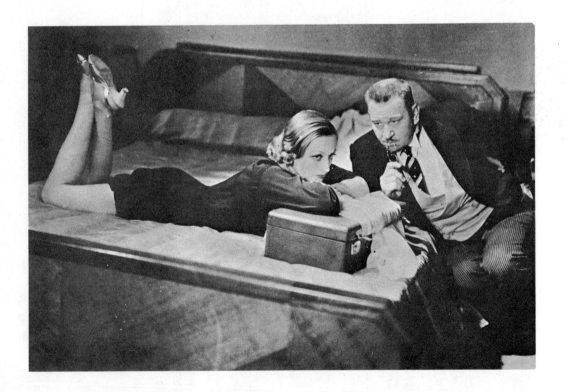

Other members of "Grand Hotel"'s glittering cast:
ABOVE: *Joan Crawford, John and Lionel Barrymore, Lewis Stone*
BELOW: *Joan Crawford and Wallace Beery*

As You Desire Me

With Erich von Stroheim

A Metro-Goldwyn-Mayer Picture (1932)

CAST

Greta Garbo, Melvyn Douglas, Erich von Stroheim, Owen Moore, Hedda Hopper, Rafaela Ottiano, Warburton Gamble, Albert Conti, William Ricciardi, Roland Varno

CREDITS

Directed by George Fitzmaurice. Adaptation and dialogue by Gene Markey from the play by Luigi Pirandello. Photography by William Daniels. Edited by George Hively.

SYNOPSIS

Zara (Greta Garbo), is a café entertainer in Budapest. She has amnesia. Tony Boffie (Owen Moore) sees her and identifies her as Maria, the wife of Count Bruno Varelli (Melvyn Douglas). Boffie, a portrait painter, had done a painting of Maria at the time of her marriage. She was believed to have been killed when the Austrians invaded Italy during the war.

Zara, wanting to escape from Carl Salter (Erich von Stroheim), a novelist who has a hypnotic influence over her, decides to go back with Boffie. Varelli accepts her as his wife and she falls in love with him.

Salter, wanting her back, brings another woman to Varelli saying Zara is an imposter, but does not succeed in his venture. Zara continues to be Varelli's wife, although she is still not certain of her true identity.

Although this was Garbo's first film with Douglas, they were to make a screen hit together years later in *Ninotchka*. *As You Desire Me* was Garbo's twentieth movie.

With Roland Varno (at right)

With Erich von Stroheim

What the critics said about
AS YOU DESIRE ME

Photoplay:

We hate to write the words, "This may be the last Garbo picture you will see," but at this moment it appears that she will not make any more now—if ever. And Garbo has never been more marvelous; never has she possessed such youthful beauty or such wistful appeal. She appears in a platinum wig, and without the wig looks like a girl of eighteen. The love scenes between Douglas and Garbo are the high points of the film, and they almost equal the ones played so long ago by Gilbert and Garbo. If this must be her last picture, we are glad it is such a fitting swan song.

J.C.M.
in *The New Yorker:*

I am inclined to think that there is altogether too much discussion of Garbo these days. It is enough to say that this is not one of her most ambitious offerings, yet by no means one of her most trivial. As you have heard, she wears a blond wig in it; but only for a moment, and I was glad when she got back to her own locks. As you have heard also, it may be her last picture. She is said to be going back to that farm of hers. Well, I shall wait and see, and occupy my mind, if possible, with other matters in the meanwhile, and try to endure the suspense. I must say, though, that the Pirandello idea of the doubtful identity which is the core of the tale—being, anyhow, a little more elaborate, we might say, than the usual movie embroilment—lifts the film above the commonplace.

With Melvyn Douglas

Queen Christina

A Metro-Goldwyn-Mayer Picture (1933)

CAST

Greta Garbo, John Gilbert, Ian Keith, Lewis Stone, Elizabeth Young, C. Aubrey Smith, Reginald Owen, Lawrence Grant, David Torrence, Gustav von Seyffertitz, Ferdinand Munier, George Renevent

CREDITS

Directed by Rouben Mamoulian. Produced by Walter Wanger. Story by Salka Viertel and Margaret F. Levin. Adapted by H. M. Harwood and Salka Viertel. Dialogue by S. N. Behrman. Photography by William Daniels. Musical score by Herbert Stothart. Edited by Blanche Sewell.

SYNOPSIS

Queen Christina of Sweden (Greta Garbo) is to marry Prince Charles (Reginald Owen), hero of the armies. Her former lover, Magnus (Ian Keith), wants the marriage arranged, knowing Christina does not love Charles. Christina, however, declines, saying she is not yet ready for marriage.

Christina learns that an ambassador from Spain, Don Antonio (John Gilbert), is to arrive. She dons boy's clothes and goes to an inn where he will stop. When Antonio learns there is no vacancy, he shares a room with Christina, thinking she is a boy. He soon realizes she is a woman, and in the next few days they fall in love.

She wants to marry him and go to Spain, but he discovers she is the Queen and tells her that he has been sent to arrange a marriage between her and the King of Spain.

When Don Antonio later meets her officially and sees her often, Magnus stirs up the populace against him. Christina sends Don Antonio away, then abdicates. When she arrives at the place where she is to meet him, she finds him dead, killed by Magnus. She leaves for Spain with his body, never to return.

Queen Christina was Garbo's twenty-first film and the first sound movie with John Gilbert. It was Gilbert's fourth and last film with Garbo. He was not successful in sound films, and died a few years later, despondent over his career. This film marked Lewis Stone's seventh and last appearance with Greta Garbo; he had made more pictures with her than any other actor.

With John Gilbert

With John Gilbert

With Elizabeth Young and C. Aubrey Smith

What the critics said about
QUEEN CHRISTINA

The New Yorker:

The Garbo film of the season, with the lady doing handsomely, though the story of old Sweden sags a bit.

Walter Ramsey
in *Modern Screen:*

Triumph for Garbo! One of the great pictures of the past few years, this historical epic makes a sustained drive for artistry. Besides, we have Garbo and Gilbert, very good indeed. One of the best scenes discloses Garbo, travelling as a man, and stopping at a wayside inn, there to be placed in the same room with a nobleman from Spain (Gilbert) because all other rooms are occupied. (No reason to censor and every reason to try). One does not resent the situation because it is so beautifully handled. The picture is an unending series of exceptional scenes, packed with fine characterizations and good direction. A triumph for Garbo, a come-back for Gilbert, with an orchid for Messrs. Stone and Keith. The production is in a class by itself, so you cannot afford to miss it.

Photoplay:

Garbo, as Sweden's stately sovereign of the seventeenth century! The magnificent Garbo, after an absence of over a year, makes a glorious reappearance on the screen. Garbo, enchanting as ever, is still enveloped by her unfathomable mystery. In the opening scenes, little Cora Sue Collins effectively impersonates Garbo as a child. The supporting cast is equal to every situation—and that's saying a lot when Garbo is creating the situations.

With Lewis Stone

The Painted Veil

FACING PAGE: *With Cecilia Parker, Beulah Bondi,*
Billy Bevan, and Jean Hersholt

BELOW: *With Herbert Marshall*

A Metro-Goldwyn-Mayer Picture (1934)

CAST

Greta Garbo, Herbert Marshall, George Brent, Warner Oland, Jean Hersholt, Beulah Bondi, Katherine Alexander, Cecilia Parker, Soo Yong, Forrester Harvey

CREDITS

Directed by Richard Boleslawski. Produced by Hunt Stromberg. Screen play by John Meehan, Salka Viertel, and Edith Fitzgerald from the novel by W. Somerset Maugham. Photography by William Daniels. Musical score by Herbert Stothart. Edited by Hugh Wynn.

SYNOPSIS

Katrin (Greta Garbo) marries Dr. Walter Fane (Herbert Marshall) and goes with him to China. His practice keeps him busy and away from her.

She meets Jack Townsend (George Brent), a diplomatic attaché, and has an affair with him. When Fane finds out, he says he is going into the interior to help stop a cholera epidemic and that Katrin must go with him, unless Townsend divorces his wife and marries her. Townsend, fearing for his career, does not commit himself.

Katrin leaves with Fane, but eventually Fane's attitude changes and he asks for her forgiveness. When his work calls for him to leave the disease-infested main city, he tells her that she may return to safety.

She stays on, however, and becomes a dedicated worker, helping the victims of cholera. Fane returns and finds her, and they both realize they are still in love. When he orders a district to be burned, to halt the spread of the disease, he is stabbed by an angry Chinese.

Townsend arrives at the same moment that Katrin learns Fane is wounded. Katrin disregards him completely and goes to her husband, vowing to bring him back to health.

This was Garbo's twenty-second film and her only film appearance with Marshall and Brent.

With Jean Hersholt and Herbert Marshall

What the critics said about
THE PAINTED VEIL

André Seenwald
in the *New York Times:*

   She is the most miraculous blend of personality
and sheer dramatic talent that the screen has ever
known and her presence in *The Painted Veil*
immediately makes it one of the season's cinema
events. Watch her stalking about with long and
nervous steps, her shoulders bent and her body
awkward with grief, while she waits to be told if her
husband will die from the coolie's dagger thrust. It is
as if all this had never been done before. Watch the
veiled terror of her face as she sits at dinner with
her husband, not knowing if he is aware of her
infidelity, or her superb gallantry when she informs
him of what it was that drove her into the arms of
his friend, of her restlessness on the bamboo porch
in Mei-Tain-Fu with the tinny phonograph, the heat
and her conscience. She shrouds all this with dignity,
making it precious and memorable.

Norbert Lusk
in *Picture Play:*

   Again Greta Garbo triumphs by the sheer beauty
of herself and her spirit over a picture that is only
tolerable because of what she gives to it. Magically,
she makes her heroine sensitive, poetic, and soulful
as only Garbo can . . . of course, it is invested with
Garbo's glamour, Cedric Gibbons's Oriental settings
and Adrian's costumes, but it is the same story and
the same set of characters which might have served
Norma Shearer or Joan Crawford in their respective
moods. . . . Garbo has never been lovelier, and her
smile is a benison.

With George Brent

Anna Karenina

ABOVE: *With Fredric March and May Robson*

FACING PAGE: *With Reginald Denny and Fredric March*

A Metro-Goldwyn-Mayer Picture (1935)

CAST

Greta Garbo, Fredric March, Freddie Bartholomew, Maureen O'Sullivan, May Robson, Basil Rathbone, Reginald Owen, Reginald Denny, Phoebe Foster, Gyles Isham, Buster Phelps, Ella Ethridge, Joan Marsh, Sidney Bracey, Cora Sue Collins, Olaf Hytten, Joe E. Tozer, Guy D'Ennery, Harry Allen, Mary Forbes

CREDITS

Directed by Clarence Brown. Produced by David O. Selznick. Screen play by Clemence Dane, Salka Viertel, and S. N. Behrman from the novel by Leo Tolstoy. Photography by William Daniels. Musical score by Herbert Stothart. Edited by Robert J. Kern.

SYNOPSIS

The setting is nineteenth-century Russia. Anna Karenina (Greta Garbo) is married to a wealthy government man, Karenin (Basil Rathbone), and has a young son, Sergei (Freddie Bartholomew). She goes to visit her brother, Stiva (Reginald Owen), to save his marriage from ruin due to other women in his life.

She meets Count Vronsky (Fredric March) and they fall in love. When she returns home, she continues to see him. She asks her husband for a divorce, but he refuses and tells her that if she becomes Vronsky's mistress, she will forfeit all claim to their son. Desperately in love, Anna goes with Vronsky anyway.

He leaves the army and at first their life together is idyllic. Soon he begins to yearn for the military life and, after an argument with Anna, joins the army again. When Anna goes to the train station to see him and make up with him, she sees his mother (May Robson) introducing him to a girl. Anna realizes she has lost everything important to her and throws herself in the path of a train.

Anna Karenina was Garbo's twenty-third film and a re-make of *Love,* in which she co-starred with John Gilbert.

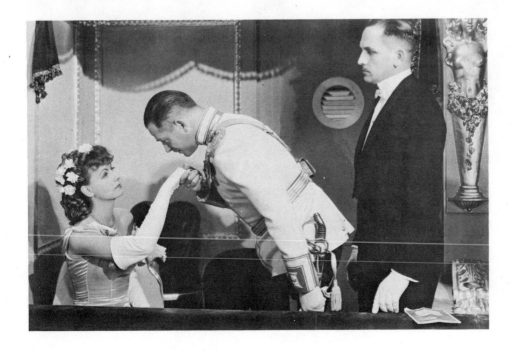

With Basil Rathbone

FACING PAGE:
(Top) With Guy D'Ennery and Freddie Bartholomew
(Bottom) With Maureen O'Sullivan

With Fredric March

With Freddie Bartholomew

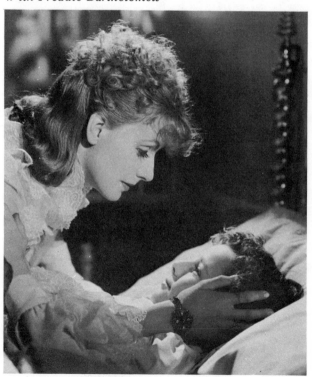

What the critics said about
ANNA KARENINA

William Boehnel
in the *New York World-Telegram:*

There is always an excitement and interest about any role that Greta Garbo portrays on the screen, and so, even though *Anna Karenina* can hardly be called one of the best films she has ever made, it is as exciting as any because of the marvelously restrained performance she gives in the title role. . . . There is nothing dull or dreary about Miss Garbo, who succeeds, for the greater part, in recreating a believable Anna.

Eileen Creelman
in the *New York Sun:*

Greta Garbo, after several years of miscasting, is back at last in her own particular province of glamor and heartbreak, of tragic lovely ladies and handsome ruthless men. She has even discarded those extraordinary costumes which have made her look like a theatrical dressmaker's advertisement, and, happily aided by excellent photography and becoming gowns, reclaimed her own unique beauty. . . . Clarence Brown may be responsible for the Swedish star's return to enchantment. It was he who directed her in *Romance*, in *Flesh and the Devil, Anna Christie*, and other of her better screen plays. After four years professionally apart, years in which Miss Garbo wandered through such dreary films as the clammy *Queen Christina*, the director-star team is reunited. For Miss Garbo's sake it may be hoped this combination will last. . . . Garbo's haunting beauty is what you will remember of *Anna Karenina*.

Photoplay:

This is a weak and dull picture, yet the persuasive genius of Garbo raises it into the class of art. What should be moving seems dated, though the production is magnificent and Garbo, exquisitely photographed, has more fire than in her last several pictures.

Nobert Lusk
in *Picture Play:*

Garbo's greatness as supreme star of the screen is here exhibited for all who have eyes to see, ears to hear, and imagination to be stirred. And, as always, the play is made to seem less important than the talent. Meticulous costumes and settings complete a marvelous reproduction of St. Petersburg society in the '70's. But dignified acting doesn't altogether disguise the Russian "East Lynne."

With Basil Rathbone and Fredric March

Camille

A Metro-Goldwyn-Mayer Picture (1937)

CAST

Greta Garbo, Robert Taylor, Lionel Barrymore, Elizabeth Allan, Jessie Ralph, Henry Daniell, Lenore Ulric, Laura Hope Crews, Rex O'Malley, Russell Hardie, E. E. Clive, Douglas Walton, Marion Ballou, Joan Brodel, June Wilkins, Fritz Leiber, Jr., Elsie Esmonds

CREDITS

Directed by George Cukor. Screen play by Zoë Akins, Frances Marion, and James Hilton from the play and novel "La Dame aux Camellias" by Alexandre Dumas. Photography by William Daniels and Karl Freund. Musical score by Herbert Stothart. Edited by Margaret Booth.

SYNOPSIS

Camille (Greta Garbo) is a fancy Parisian courtesan, whose current lover is Baron de Varville (Henry Daniell). Camille's nature is not vicious. She is kind to those who have befriended her; she even pays for the wedding of an old friend, Nichette (Elizabeth Allan).

One day at the theatre, Camille meets young Armand Duval (Robert Taylor) and both fall deeply in love. Camille wishes to spend time in the country with Armand, but the Baron finds out that she is cheating on him. He slaps her, but gives her the money she asked for.

In the country her happiness comes to an abrupt end when Armand's father (Lionel Barrymore) comes to see her alone. He tells her that if Armand marries her, he will ruin his career and his whole life. To save Armand, Camille leaves him, telling him she prefers the rich men in Paris.

Camille contracts tuberculosis, is forced to sell all her possessions, and has only her faithful maid, Nanine (Jessie Ralph), to look after her.

Dying, she cannot forget Armand. When he learns of her condition, he comes to see her and promises to stay with her forever. Camille dies, but happy in knowing that Armand still loves her.

Camille was Garbo's twenty-fourth motion picture and the only with Robert Taylor. It was Lionel Barrymore's fourth and final role in a Garbo film.

Garbo was nominated for an Academy Award for her performance in this picture.

With Henry Daniell

*With Henry Daniell,
Lenore Ulric,
and Robert Taylor*

With Eily Malyon and Robert Taylor

What the critics said about
CAMILLE

Frank S. Nugent
in the *New York Times:*

Greta Garbo's performance is in the finest tradition: eloquent, tragic, yet restrained. She is as incomparable in the role as legend tells us that Bernhardt was. Through the perfect artistry of her portrayal, a hackneyed theme is made new again, poignantly sad, hauntingly lovely . . . Miss Garbo has interpreted Marguerite Gautier with the subtlety that has earned her the title, "first lady of the screen." Even as the impish demi-mondaine of the early sequences, she has managed to convey the impression of maturity, of a certain etherealism and spiritual integrity which raise her above her surroundings and mark her as one apart . . . To appreciate her complete command of the role, one need only study her approach to the key scenes of the drama. Where the less sentient Camille bides her time until the moment comes for her to tear her passions and the scenery to tatters, Garbo waits and then understates. It is her dignity that gives strength to her scene with M. Duval when he asks her to give up his son. It is because her emotions do not slip their leash—when you feel that any second they might—that saves her parting scene with Armand from being a cliche renunciation. And, above all, it is her performance in the death scene—so simply, delicately and movingly played—which convinces me that Camille is Garbo's best performance.

Howard Barnes
in the *New York Herald Tribune:*

The incomparable Greta Garbo has returned to the screen in a breathtakingly beautiful and superbly modulated portrayal of *Camille*. As the tragic Dumas heroine, she floods a romantic museum piece with glamor and artistry, making it a haunting and moving photoplay by the sheer magic of her acting. It was not my good fortune to witness the great Eleanora Duse in the play, but I have seen many other illustrious actresses in French and English versions, and none have remotely matched Miss Garbo . . . She dignifies this latest of many presentations of *Camille* with a magnificent and unforgettable performance.

There has been no diminution of Miss Garbo's flaming genius during her recent absence from motion picture acting. Her command of the subtleties of an impersonation is even greater than it was in the past, and her voice has taken on a new range of inflection. The Marguerite she brings to the screen is not only the errant and self-sacrifical nymph conceived by the younger Dumas nearly a hundred years ago, but one of the timeless figures of all great art. With fine intelligence and unerring instinct she has made her characterization completely credible, while giving it an aching poignancy that, to me, is utterly irresistible. She achieves a consummate balance between the conflicting qualities that made up the eighteenth century demi-mondaine, and she plays the big flamboyant scenes of the piece with a versatile intensity that unshackles them from all their creaking artificiality and fills them with brooding emotional power and ineffable splendor . . . It is likely that Miss Garbo still has her greatest role to play, but she has made the Lady of the Camelias, for this reviewer, hers for all time.

With Henry Daniell,
Rex O'Malley, Jessie Ralph,
and Laura Hope Crews

FACING PAGE:
With Lionel Barrymore

Conquest

With Charles Boyer

A Metro-Goldwyn-Mayer Picture (1937)

CAST

Greta Garbo, Charles Boyer, Reginald Owen, Alan Marshall, Henry Stephenson, Leif Erickson, Dame May Whitty, C. Henry Gordon, Vladimir Sokoloff, Maria Ouspenskaya, Scotty Beckett

CREDITS

Directed by Clarence Brown. Produced by Bernard H. Hyman. Screen play by Samuel Hoffenstein, Salka Viertel, and S. N. Behrman from the novel "Pani Walewska" by Waclaw Gasiorowski and a dramatization by Helen Jerome. Photography by Karl Freund. Musical score by Herbert Stothart. Edited by Tom Held.

SYNOPSIS

In 1807, Napoleon Bonaparte (Charles Boyer) visits Poland. At a state ball, he sees Countess Marie Walewska (Greta Garbo) and is attracted to her. When she is asked by Poland's leaders to visit Napoleon to gain his aid in making Poland independent, she reluctantly agrees.

She has an affair with him, and when her husband, Count Walewski (Henry Stephenson), finds out, he divorces her. Marie becomes Napoleon's mistress and leaves with him. However, she sees him losing his love for her and the cause of freedom and, in its stead, gaining a love for power. She hopes to marry him, but when Talleyrand (Reginald Owen) arranges his marriage to the Hapsburg princess Marie Louise, her hopes are gone.

Marie Walewska bears Napoleon a son. After Napoleon's defeat at Waterloo, she takes their son to see him. Marie and Napoleon say their last farewells before he is taken into exile at St. Helena.

Conquest was Garbo's twenty-fifth film, and the only one with Charles Boyer.

With Henry Stephenson

What the critics said about
CONQUEST

John Mosher
in *The New Yorker:*

   Madame Garbo's elegant anemia, I fear, can pall a
little. Her performance seems static, though the story
covers a period of years. Beautiful, fragile, and
tired, she stands in the first scene among the Cossacks
invading her husband's house; and quite unchanged,
fragile and tired still, she waves her last farewell
to Napoleon, as though she would assert and try to
prove that loyalty is but a symptom of exhaustion.
I think that for the first time Madame Garbo has a
leading man who contributes more to the interest and
vitality of the film than she does. She is, we may
assume, grateful for such assistance.

With Scotty Beckett and Charles Boyer

Ninotchka

A Metro-Goldwyn-Mayer Picture (1939)

CAST

Greta Garbo, Melvyn Douglas, Ina Claire, Bela Lugosi, Sig Rumann, Felix Bressart, Alexander Granach, Gregory Gaye, Rolfe Sedan, Edwin Maxwell, Richard Carle

CREDITS

Produced and directed by Ernst Lubitsch. Story by Melchior Lengyel. Screen play by Charles Brackett, Billy Wilder and Walter Reisch. Photography by William Daniels. Musical score by Werner R. Heymann. Edited by Gene Ruggiero.

SYNOPSIS

Iranoff (Sig Rumann), Buljanoff (Felix Bressart), and Kopalski (Alexander Granach) are sent by the Soviet Government to Paris to sell jewels and use the money for farm machinery. However, the Grand Duchess Swana (Ina Claire), who owned the jewels before she fled to France, has a court injunction filed to prevent the sale. Her boy friend, Leon (Melvyn Douglas), does this and also introduces the three Russians to Parisian life.

Hearing of the delay, the Soviet Government sends Ninotchka (Greta Garbo) to straighten out matters, and she finds her comrades leading a gay life in Paris. The three men ask Leon to help them. Leon had met Ninotchka already, unaware of her identity at first, but drawn to her. Leon begins seeing her regularly, and she not only thaws out and drops her stern manner, but falls in love with him and he with her.

However, when a waiter working for Swana steals the jewels, Swana agrees to give up her rights to them if Ninotchka will return to Russia. Leon finds out, but cannot get a passport to follow her to Russia.

Iranoff, Buljanoff, and Kopalski also have returned to Russia, and have been sent to sell furs in Constantinople. Commissar Razinin (Bela Lugosi) sends Ninotchka there to aid them. When she arrives, she learns that the three men plan to stay there and open a restaurant. They had told Leon that she was coming. Leon persuades her to stay with him and be his wife.

Ninotchka was Garbo's twenty-sixth film and her second with Melvyn Douglas. It was her first American comedy role. She was nominated for an Academy Award for this performance.

Garbo laughs

FACING PAGE:
(Top) With Sig Rumann, Felix Blessart, and Alexander Granach
(Left) With Ina Claire
(Right) With Melvyn Douglas

With Melvyn Douglas

What the critics said about
NINOTCHKA

Howard Barnes
in the *New York Herald Tribune:*

Now that she has done it, it seems incredible that Greta Garbo never apeared in a comedy before *Ninotchka*. For in this gay burlesque of Bolsheviks abroad, the great actress reveals a command of comic inflection which fully matches the emotional depth or tragic power of her earlier triumphs. It is a joyous, subtly shaded and utterly enchanting portrayal which she creates, to illuminate a rather slight satire and make it the year's most captivating screen comedy. Ernst Lubitsch has put his famous directorial touch on the film and it is leavened with witty lines and deft characterizations, but it is memorable as well as entertaining for having disclosed new gifts in the First Actress of our day.

To see Garbo playing a grim comrade who deviates from party doctrine on a mission to Paris, turns square briefly, and then goes overboard for romance, one would suppose that she had devoted her whole career to antic make-believe. Whether it is deadpan clowning or the difficult feat of filling a tipsy scene with laughter; whether she is trading insults with a Grand Duchess or secretly trying on one of those current hats, she is a past mistress of comedy. Meanwhile, she floods the production with her timeless and ineffable beauty, giving a rich and haunting quality to the romantic scenes and a moving intensity to the few passages of straight drama. There is an added verve and color to her personality in a role such as this which makes her even more magically lovely than in the past.

Frank S. Nugent
in the *New York Times:*

Garbo's *Ninotchka* is one of the sprightliest comedies of the year, a gay and impertinent and malicious show which never pulls the punch lines (no matter how far below the belt they may land) and finds the screen's austere first lady of drama playing in deadpan comedy with the assurance of a Buster Keaton. . . . It must be monotonous, this superb rightness of Garbo's playing. We almost wish she would handle a scene badly once in a while just to provide us with an opportunity to show we are not a member of a fan club. But she remains infallible and Garbo, always exactly what the situation demands, always as fine as her script and director permit her to be.

*With Sig Rumann,
Felix Blessart, and
Alexander Granach*

With Melvyn Douglas

Two-Faced Woman

A Metro-Goldwyn-Mayer Picture (1941)

CAST

  Greta Garbo, Melvyn Douglas, Constance Bennett, Roland Young,
Robert Sterling, Ruth Gordon, Francis Carson

CREDITS

  Directed by George Cukor. Produced by Gottfried Reinhardt. Screen
play by S. N. Behrman, Salka Viertel, and George Oppenheimer from
the play by Ludwig Fulda. Photography by Joseph Ruttenberg. Musical
score by Bronislau Kaper. Edited by George Boemler.

SYNOPSIS

  Larry Blake (Melvyn Douglas), publisher of a news magazine, goes
to a ski resort on vacation. He meets and marries Karin (Greta Garbo),
a ski instructress there. Larry promises Karin to give up his sophisticated
New York life, and returns to the city alone.

  His ex-flame, Griselda Vaughn (Constance Bennett), plots to get him
back. Unknown to anyone, Karin arrives in New York and sees she
cannot compete with the glamorous Griselda. To combat Griselda,
Karin impersonates her own twin, a gay and worldly-wise woman. Larry
realizes it is really Karin and tries to get her to expose herself.

  When he makes love to her, she realizes her plans have backfired.
She returns to the ski resort. Larry follows her, proves to her that he
was on to her disguise, and they are reconciled.

  Two-Faced Woman was Garbo's twenty-seventh and final film. Melvyn
Douglas appeared opposite her for the third time in this second of her
American comedies.

ABOVE:
*With Melvyn Douglas
and Roland Young*

With Constance Bennett

With Melvyn Douglas

What the critics said about
TWO-FACED WOMAN

in the *New York Times:*

As for Miss Garbo, this is clearly one of the less propitious assignments of her career. Though she is her cool and immaculate self in the role of the clean-limbed ski instructress, she is as gauche and stilted as the script when playing the lady of profane love. No doubt her obvious posturings, her appallingly unflattering clothes and make-up were intended as a satire on the vamps of history; instead, her performance misses the satire and looks like something straight out of the movies of 1922. Mr. Douglas, who probably spends more time in pyjamas than any male lead in history, continues to look as though a brisk walk in the open air in street clothes would refresh him. Apply that rule to the whole film. Open the windows, Messrs. Cukor, Behrman, Oppenheimer, et al. This is 1942, and Theda Bara's golden age is gone.

Time:

An absurd vehicle for Greta Garbo. . . . Its embarrassing effect is not unlike seeing Sarah Bernhardt swatted with a bladder. It is almost as shocking as seeing your mother drunk.

Cecilia Ager
in the newspaper *PM:*

The screen doesn't have an actress to compare with Garbo for loveliness, sensitivity, incandescence. She has feeling first, and she's acquired the technical proficiency and the knack of timing with which to express it. In *Two-Faced Woman* she reveals still deeper stores of humor and evanescent tenderness than ever before. Her voice has become an instrument that indicates all the emotions in their most subtle gradations. Just on the record of the sound track she's superb. And this is the woman, so unique in the movies that she's no longer a person but become now a symbol, a legend, whom *Two-Faced Woman* does everything it can to destroy. The wickedness in *Two-Faced Woman* was not in its careless disregard of what are supposed to be public morals—it had no more contempt for the conventions than a half-dozen recent movies for whose transgressions it was made an example of—its wickedness lies in its vandalism. In its story's frenzy to cover up its own emptiness, its sterility, its lack of any fine feelings, it makes Garbo a clown, a buffoon, a monkey on a stick. The fact that it's a comedy doesn't excuse its confused motivation, its repetition, its distasteful heartlessness.

With Constance Bennett and Melvyn Douglas

With Melvyn Douglas